"He Knows Faith"

· ST. JOHN'S STORIES ·

"He Knows Faith"

ST. JOHN'S STORIES

Michael J. Moran

"He Knows Faith": St. John's Stories

ISBN-13: 978-1542862035

ISBN-10: 1542862035

Print and Kindle editions available through Amazon.

For more about other books by the author, please visit

MICHAELJMORAN.WEBS.COM

• THANKS •

*to Cathy Moran
for excellent suggestions and editing*

• DEDICATION •

*to Mike and Al and Charlie and Ray
and all the other guys who made
the experience unforgettable*

1 • THE SEM

So what was I going to be: a potential priest or a college basketball player? Those misaligned possibilities were mine in the spring of 1961. The priestly option had been flitting about in my brain during the spring of my senior year of high school. My guess is that virtually every Catholic boy of that era gave at least a few moments to imagining himself as a priest. My grade school teachers, all of them nuns, encouraged us to consider the lofty vocation, and those who, like me, attended a high school with many priest-teachers had their good example before us on a daily basis. And so, around March or April, I thought I had reached a decision: I would give St. John's Seminary, in my hometown of Little Rock, Arkansas, a try.

But then came the secular temptation: an offer of what I then called a "basketball scholarship." I've since decided that "scholarship" usually had, at that time, and still has little or nothing to do with being a scholar. I now insist in saying, "athletic grant-in-aid" whenever referring to such arrangements between colleges and athletes. My present Puritanical preference aside, a college coach wanted me to play my favorite sport!

Not only was I being courted by a local coach, Bill Ballard, the head of the Little Rock University Trojans, but I also received a letter making inquiry about my interest in playing for another college, Pittsburg State in Pittsburg, Kansas. I was floored at being "recruited" (a word I wouldn't have used in 1961) by another team, but when I read further into the note, I discovered that the Pittsburg sports teams were known then—as now—as the "Gorillas." Standing 5'9" and weighing about 145 pounds, the only way that I would ever hear myself described as a "Gorilla" would be in a tone of voice heavy with sarcasm. I passed on Pittsburg.

My interest in going to the seminary wasn't a secret, though I don't remember telling anyone. One or two priests on the faculty of my school, Catholic High School for Boys, encouraged me to take the step. Despite their urging, sometime after graduation I made a decision: basketball.

I lasted about two weeks at L.R.U. before deciding that I had made a mistake. Classes were fine; the basketball practices were fun, but something was missing. Was it too late to go to St. John's? Dad inquired on my behalf. No, it was not too late. I approached Coach Ballard and told him I was headed for the seminary, and he was most gracious and wished me the best. It's possible that what he saw of my basketball skills in those couple of weeks of practice made my departure less than painful.

My parents, Grace and Ray Moran, were as agreeable as one could hope his parents to be when zig-zagging about one's future. A couple of days were spent preparing to leave for the seminary and going to the Guardian Church Goods store to buy the necessities for being a seminarian: the long, robe-like black cassock: the white, blouse-like surplice; and the four-sided, three-pronged black cap known as a biretta. Once that was all acquired, it was off to St. John's Home Missions Seminary, sometime in late September.

Notification and Warning: In what follows, I hope to relate accurately what happened and what was said, but I am aware that my memory is sometimes shaky and my imagination is sometimes overactive. Also, while it's true that for the most part the stories are lighthearted, there were serious moments aplenty; my goal, however, is to entertain, so the serious stuff is left to be told another day.

FIDEM SCIT

11 • FIFTH PREP

My classmates in "fifth prep" as the freshmen in college were known (there being four lower levels, the high school seminarians) numbered about eighteen. Four or five of them had been high-schoolers at St. John's; the rest of us were new. There was one class of college sophomores in our building ("prep side") as well; the six groups of students thus constituted the preparatory seminary. The last six years' worth of seminarians lived on the "the "upper side" of the three-building complex that made up the entire seminary. We were the "minor" seminarians, and they were the "major." The third building was the refectory, or eating hall, that also housed three nuns who did all the cooking for what probably amounted to more than 160 students daily, plus the faculty of about ten priests.

When I arrived at the fifth prep dormitory, which might have been 600 square feet, three walls were filled with bunk beds; the fourth wall had no beds because it was alongside the entryway to the dorm. In the middle of the room was one single bed:

I quickly figured out whose it was. To say that I felt self-conscious about being late to join fifth prep is absolutely true. To say that sleeping in the middle of the room with all eyes (I imagined) on me making me even more self-conscious is even truer.

But my fellow seminarians quickly made me feel at home. As a matter of fact, three of them had been high school classmates. Mike O'Malley I had known since the fourth grade and with whom I played both football and basketball as Wabbits at our grade school, Holy Souls; Charlie Lipsmeyer and Jerry Sweetman I had known at Catholic High since the 9th grade. It didn't take long for me to get accustomed to the routine at St. John's: rising at 6:00 under a condition known as "grand silence," that had begun the night before when lights went out at 10:00, and it lasted until a bell was rung after saying grace before breakfast (which itself followed a period of meditation and Mass in the prep side chapel). To speak during grand silence was an offense against the intent of the practice, which was to foster a prayerful state of mind. Penalties existed for breaking grand silence.

Grand silence played a part in a prank that was played on me not long after my arrival. A bell would ring about 9:50 each night to let us all know that grand silence was approaching, so tooth-brushing and last visits to porcelain facilities could be made. The dormitory light was turned off when the bell rang again at 10:00, but it wasn't uncommon for boys to still be in the lighted hallways hurrying back from their nightly ministrations when the bell sounded.

How the pranksters knew I would return to the dorm under those darkened conditions, I don't know. Maybe I had habitually arrived after the light was extinguished. Anyway, their timing was perfect. On this night, when the bell for grand silence rang, I was late getting to the dorm, so the room was dark when I entered, with just enough visibility to see the bare outlines of my bed. I pulled away the sheet and got in, only to find my bed occupied by something—something nearly bed-length and quite hard.

"What the heck?" I said—or maybe "hell," I can't recall—but I did say something, and on cue, Ray Linder, who was the "senior man" (the first boy, four years before, to enroll in the class) and who was in charge of discipline matters such as enforcing grand silence, announced for all to hear that I had broken grand silence and some punishment would follow. What also followed was lots of laughter and someone else, also according to plan, turned on the lights so I could see that a large statue of the Blessed Virgin was in my bed, and, as the last step in the process, two of my classmates then stepped forward to help me carry it to wherever it had been sitting on a pedestal. I had to laugh myself at the cleverness and the timing, and I suppose that amounted to my initiation into fifth prep and paying the price for tardily joining up.

*

Another event that took place in the last ten minutes before lights-out and the start of grand silence involved one classmate's nightly prayer ritual. James was one of the "veterans" who had been in the seminary high school. My first impression of him was that he was formal rather than friendly, and extremely serious and religious. When I contrasted my estimate of my own "spirituality," as it was commonly called, with his, I knew I wasn't in his league. If a seminarian had to be as religious as he was, I'd never make it.

Each night when the bell rang ten minutes before grand silence, James would hustle out of the room. One night, out in the hall myself, I noticed him not only exiting the dorm into the hallway, but he took a half-flight of stairs down to the door that led outside. On a couple of nights more I saw him do that again before I asked one of the other veterans where James was going each night.

I was asked if I had seen "the grotto." I had. It was located in a woodsy area not far from the door by which James left the building. A small creek ran through the area, and sometime in the past the seminarians had built a small platform of concrete and rock taken from the woods. A kneeler that could withstand the elements was placed on the platform. The kneeler faced a recess dug into an earthen wall, and an oblong rock and mortar covering for the statue of the Blessed Virgin was installed. It was to this place that James went each night, I was told, to say his final prayers of the day. That such an idea concerning prayer would never occur to me was further proof that if James was what a seminarian was supposed to be, I had a long way to go.

One night James left the dorm for his usual, last-minute encounter with the "B.V.M.," as I commonly heard her called— an acronym that invariably signaled familiarity rather than lack of respect. Laughter and knowing looks were exchanged after he left the dorm. "What's going on?" asked one of my classmates, as much in the dark as I was. "We'll tell you later. Just keep an eye on him when he comes back." And so we did. When he came through the door, which he did with great rapidity, he looked stricken, or aghast, or maybe even scared. A minute later, the lights-out bell sounded; we would have to wait until morning for an explanation.

Sometime the next day I heard the story. James was, as I said, overtly religious, and at St. John's, perhaps oddly enough, such public displays were frowned upon. If I were to describe what I saw over time as the outward signs of spirituality of the great majority of the seminarians it was this: little or nothing. "Keep your holiness to yourself" seemed to be the seminary motto. My assumption that James' apparent devotion was the norm turned out to be the exact opposite of the reality. So, the night that James returned to the dorm shaken was the night that some who took exception to his behavior had acted.

How many were involved I don't know, but it had to be several, because they removed the statue, which might have been almost five feet tall and surely weighed hundreds of pounds. The grotto wasn't lighted at night other than what stars and moon could offer. Witnesses in hiding later testified that when James took his position on the kneeler was the moment when the high schooler who was hiding under a sheet in the spot where the statue previously stood began to moan, "James, James."

The witnesses noted that the retreat was sudden, and we who saw the look on his face and the speed in James' step as he re-entered the dorm could verify the effect it had on him. Though James didn't seem much changed by the visit to the grotto in terms of his personal formality or outward religiosity, one thing did change. His grotto visits ceased.

*

Mike O'Malley, on his first day at St. John's, witnessed another seminarian's interesting step away from the life he had led prior to entering the seminary. Having checked in late on the initial day to report, Mike missed supper (what we later would describe as "a lucky break"). Mike came across two kindred, tardy newcomers, and the three of them took a walk in "the neighborhood," as the houses around the seminary became known to one and all. Making their way back to St. John's, one, whom I shall call L.D., reached into the pocket of the coat he was wearing and withdrew a half-pint liquor bottle, opened it, and took an emptying snort. As the imbiber was about to re-enter the seminary grounds, he tossed the bottle in some nearby weeds, saying, "Well, I guess that's the end of that."

*

I can say precisely that it was on the afternoon of September 29th that I heard a bell, the small one that was used at Mass, but its sound came from outside the fifth prep dorm. Several windows of our dorm looked out on the oval drive that cars used to get to the three seminary buildings. A sidewalk paralleled the drive, and there I saw four young, young seminarians—boys I recognized as ninth graders.

The bell-ringer was first in the group, all of whom were wearing cassocks (black robes) and surplices (loose, white, wide-sleeved, shirt-like vestments). Following the bellboy was a lad carrying a large cross attached to a pole—perhaps four feet long in all. Following him were two candle bearers, their lit candles in long holders. It didn't take long for others in the dorm to notice the parade, and one or more of our veterans happily described what was happening. September 29, as we had heard that morning at Mass, was the feast day of Michael the Archangel. What was occurring was a St. John's tradition, which like many of them, as I was to find out over time, was a put-on, a hoax, a prank. By any name, deceptions were commonplace.

The foursome had been solemnly told by their senior man—the first among equals who was a senior in high school—that they were to go to the upper side to get the relic (an object considered holy because of its association with a saint) of St. Michael the Archangel—a feather. They were then to bring it to the prep side chapel. Their destination was a room on the upper side wherein lived the oldest priest on campus, Monsignor Edward Garrity. Monsignor Garrity was a delightful man well into his eighties, and he lived in what I would imagine was a pleasant retirement, except for those times when he was involuntarily involved in seminary shenanigans. This was such a time.

The vets in our dorm told us what would happen: The quartet would enter the upper side and be escorted by one or more "helpful" major seminarians to Monsignor Garrity's hall, at the end of which were his living quarters. The boys would be instructed to knock on his door and request the feather to take to prep side.

Monsignor's hall was also populated by several student rooms, the doors to which were all open to permit those within to hear the anticipated conversation. We were told that Monsignor Garrity would invariably fuss at the boys for not knowing that there was no such thing as a feather relic of a spiritual creature such as an angel. He'd then tell them to go back to prep side and leave him alone.

From the look of the returning ninth graders, the veterans' predictions about what would happen certainly proved true. We soon saw the four boys coming back in no particular order, the candles extinguished, the cross being lowered, and unhappy looks all around. I realize now that I should have made a mental note following James' encounter in the grotto and this charade involving a feather, to remember that often at St. John's things were not what they seemed.

*

The guys at St. John's loved Monsignor Garrity, but his excitable nature apparently proved an irresistible target. When the lights-out bell rang, Monsignor Garrity wanted all the residents of the rooms along his hall to be out of the hallway, and to stay out. The fact that there was a small bathroom on his hallway didn't mean, in his mind, that it should be used after grand silence had begun, regardless of the volume and intensity of nature's call. When he heard someone opening the toilet's door, he'd exit his room and open the same door just a touch, scolding the person within and telling him to get back to his room. It was the price one paid for using the room before Monsignor was asleep. It must have irritated one or more of the hall's residents. What follows happened before I entered St. John's.

pre-1961: Conspirators decided to put the old priest to the test. Just before 10:00, in one of the closed toilets on his corridor, a toilet whose sides stopped perhaps 18 inches from the floor, a space that was visible from the door, they assembled what would have looked like, to someone standing at the door, the shoes and rumpled pants of a person sitting on the toilet. That's what Monsignor Garrity saw when he opened the door soon after one of the hall's residents noisily pretended to enter the toilet and then quickly and quietly high-tailed it back to his room.

The pranksters were no doubt at their doors, listening intently as Monsignor Garrity was heard opening the door and telling the shoes-and-pants guy to hurry up and leave. Back in his room, the priest was waiting to hear the door open as the culprit left the toilet. When it didn't happen, Monsignor returned once, and then twice, and then a third time to further complain about the fellow's refusal to leave. He gave up at that point, his threats to report the recalcitrant one to the rector going unheeded. The shoes and pants were then spirited away.

*

In another year, high jinks involving Monsignor Garrity reached a perfect-timing peak. His dislike of hearing any sounds in his hallway after lights-out was the focus of a plan. As he sat in his room one night, post-ten-o'clock, he heard a rumble in the hall unlike, I'm sure, anything he had ever heard before or thereafter. I mentioned that he was an octogenarian, so he probably took at least a few seconds before he could rise from his chair, walk to the door and open it. When he got there, whatever had made the earth-shaking sound was not there. I assume he never found out what happened.

What had happened was that at the end of the hallway most distant from Monsignor's room, at, say, 10:04 on one of two synchronized watches, a seminarian stepped out of his room and rolled a bowling ball down the hall towards Monsignor Garrity's door. His accomplice, in the room next to Monsignor Garrity's, opened his door at the first sound of the approaching ball, silently stepped out into the *hall and gathered up the sphere just before it got to the Garrity door and before the befuddled priest could open it. Taking the ball inside he placed it in his closet, probably behind his suitcase, and made a mental note to return it to his classmate the following day when Monsignor Garrity was saying Mass. You'll have to decide if an old man's desire to prohibit visits to a toilet deserved such responses.*

*

The courses we took in fifth prep were mostly like those that other college freshmen were taking, though most of them who were taking a foreign language weren't studying Latin, as we all were. In 1961 the Second Vatican Council that changed many things about the Catholic Church was a year away, so the Latin Mass was still a worldwide phenomenon, regardless of the native tongue in common use where the Mass was celebrated. Everyone in fifth prep was taking Latin, though some were more advanced than others. The boys who had been at St. John's throughout high school already had studied four years of it. Those of us who were newcomers had mostly gone to Catholic high schools, where at least two years of Latin were common. Albert Schneider, known to all as Al, was a four-year Latin letterman, and he really knew his stuff, so much so that he became a vital part of the Latin learning experience for those of us who lagged behind him in our knowledge. He assisted Father James Drane (about whom, considerably more to come), our Latin teacher, by making tapes that we listened to in our "language lab," a modern (or so it seemed to us at the time) method of teaching a foreign language by providing individual booths with headsets that allowed us to hear Al's Latin recitations of common stories and biblical tales that might make the foreign language seem less foreign. I hope if Al ever reads these words he'll not be upset to know that the sentence I best remember (the only sentence I remember?) that he spoke often enough that it actually remains in my head was, "Maria habuit parvum agnum." Even had you not a single day in Latin, you probably have an idea that those words have something to do with a gal named Mary and a small pet that she owned.

*

One of the classes that was also probably unlike those taken by our fellow freshmen in secular colleges was Church History. The teacher tended to read out of the text. Truth be told, he *only* read out of the text. If you have ever been in such a class, I need say no more about the scintillation factor which that approach produces. The classrooms at St. John's were located on prep side, where we lived, and the one in which Church History met had about thirty desks in it. Since we had no more than 20 in fifth prep, there were vacant desks aplenty. We could sit wherever we liked, so it happened that one day, the aforementioned L.D., he of the tossed liquor bottle, seated himself in the last row, with no one else nearby. His choice would have probably gone unnoticed and unremarked had he not fallen victim to the effect that text-reading often produces: Sleep. Since the teacher had his head down—reading, of course—L.D.'s snoozing would have not aroused his notice, until the snoring began. It was not muffled, fuzzy-sounding snoring; it was snoring that brings to mind the ring, the matador, and the bull.

Every head turned toward the buzz-saw or the eighteen-wheeler or whatever it was that had somehow barged its way into the room. None could shake L.D.'s shoulder or kick his desk. He was on that island of his own making in the last row—totally out of reach. I see that I said, "every" head, and that needs correcting: every head but one. The reader read on, undeterred by the acoustical interruption. Did he not hear it, so absorbed was he in the reading material? Did he refuse to admit to himself, much less his students, that he had provoked a degree of somnolence so pronounced that it seemed as if the glass in the windows would soon begin to rattle? Unanswerable questions.

Eventually another sound could be heard by all present—other than the reader, of course—stifled laughter wafted back and forth for the few minutes of class that remained. By the time the class was over, and the reader had retired from the room, we virtually ached from the restraints we had been putting on ourselves to contain the hilarity. Just for fun, we left the room without waking him up.

*

pre-1961: An elderly priest still in residence when I arrived had, a couple years before, gotten assistance from one of my classmates, the aforementioned Al Schneider. Al helped Father John Mulligan with, among other things, tidying up his quarters. Father Mulligan was a prolific consumer of cigarettes, so emptying ash trays was a common duty for Al. Winston was the priest's favorite, a popular, filter-tipped brand. While Al was about to empty a tray, Father Mulligan noticed something odd about its contents. "Albert, you don't smoke do you?" Al said he did not. The priest was staring intently at the cigarette butts, trying to unravel a mystery there. He finally solved the fact that five of the butts had filters and two did not. Laughing, he cackled, "I must have smoked the filters of these two!"

*

Father Mulligan had retired from teaching by the time I got to St. John's, but he liked being around us seminarians and especially enjoyed hearing the guitar playing of Bill Cingolani, who was in sixth prep. "Cing," as he was invariably called, would play songs that many of us knew, and a songfest would ensue. While listening one day, Father Mulligan made a request: "Cing, can you play 'I've Got Ants in My Pants and Chiggers on My Hiney?'" We were sorry that he didn't know the tune. We would have urged Father Mulligan to sing it for us.

*

In the fall of our year in fifth prep, those of us who were called "new men" (despite the fact that we were all about 18 and still legally "boys") were alerted to something that was coming: the Gaudete Sunday Speech Contest. *Gaudete* is Latin for "rejoice," and it was the first word of the readings (in Latin, of course) for the third Sunday in Advent, which would be December 17th.

The word that the "old men" circulated about the contest was thrilling to hear. On that third Sunday in Advent, all the seminary would assemble in the auditorium to hear the speeches, which were to be based on any or all of that day's readings at Mass, such as the epistle or gospel. Not only would all the seminarians be in attendance, so too would be the faculty, and, yes, our rector, Monsignor James O'Connell. And I should also mention that the head of the diocese of Little Rock himself, Bishop Albert J. Fletcher, would be the main guest!

If that wasn't enough incentive to try to shine, the fact that a prize would be awarded to the champion added to the motivation. We new men were told that the previous year's first-place prize had been a "hi-fi," which, for those readers not of a certain age, was a stereo record player—a device for playing music.

It didn't take long before evidence aplenty was visible among my fifth prep comrades that all of us but the handful of old men were working on our speeches. If one passed by another new man writing at his desk, he'd put his arm over the paper or suddenly draw it into his lap. New men could be seen walking, paper in hand, to empty classrooms wherein the practice of the potential prize-winner could occur. Like the others, I was composing what I hoped would be a winner. I had been given a small part to play as a public speaker at our graduation, so that experience would probably be advantageous. I decided, however, not to follow this time the advice that Father George Tribou had given me and the other graduation speakers, advice that I followed, which was that the wearing of a jock strap would lessen one's nerves. I have to admit that the strap worked in the sense that the binding nature of its function, on a hot night made hotter by the wearing of a graduation gown, distracted me from all other concerns. But, as I said, for Gaudete I wasn't going that far.

As I mentally sized up the competition, my old pal Mike O'Malley looked like a dangerous competitor. At Catholic High in Father George Tribou's English class, we, like hundreds before and after us at C.H.S., had to memorize and recite a part of a long, epic poem by Stephen Vincent Benet called *John*

Brown's Body. At least a generation of Father Tribou's students will recall the opening words of the excerpt, "Fall of the possum, fall of the 'coon."

Father Tribou called each of us to come to the front of the room and say the words from memory. The number of lines required I can't recall, but it seemed like a lot. When it was Mike's turn, he ripped into the first few lines but then got lost and stopped. Father Tribou told him he'd get a second chance on another day. On his second try, Mike amazed us, not merely by getting all the words in all the right places, but also by the impassioned approach he took. He was emoting; he was feeling it! When he finished, Father Tribou, as stunned as the rest of us, complimented Mike on his great recovery and for daring to put his heart into his recitation.

I don't know if that public moment had anything to do with Mike's decision to try out for the school play—*You Can't Take It with You*— that spring, but try out he did, and he landed the choice part of Martin Vanderhof, a wise, caring, funny grandfather. Mike was outstanding in the play; everybody who saw it said so. So as I contemplated the field of obstacles between me and that year's prize, Mike was clearly at the top of my list. More than once, as December drew nigh and then arrived, I passed closed classroom doors and heard him within, speechifying. Despite our long connection of ten years, I would have to try my best to top him.

Finally, Gaudete Sunday—a day to rejoice in all Christian communities because of the proximity of Christmas—was upon us. As night fell and we all headed for the auditorium, I felt the stomach buzz that I associated with the tip-off of a basketball game. As it happened, Mike and I sat next to each other. The new men were seated in the row right behind the faculty. The bishop's chair was prominently placed in the middle of that row. The emcee took the stage, standing behind a lectern. The only other thing on the stage was a table, on top of which was a large box, shiny in blue wrapping paper, with a white bow at the top. It looked to me like a container big enough to hold a hi-fi.

The emcee said that Bishop Fletcher was running late and that he didn't want to delay the contest. He would be there shortly. Speakers would be chosen randomly—names drawn from a hat. The first was selected. Judging each speech one-by-one, I really didn't think any of them was riveting. Too often the speaker was so clearly nervous that one's attention was taken from the subject matter and presentation to just hoping the contestant could get through the ordeal. Notes were permitted, but that didn't always alleviate the nerves.

As the speeches continued, I was aware that he whom I saw as my major competition, the aforementioned O'Malley, hadn't been called. Nor had I. The speeches marched on. When the emcee announced that because of time constraints, not all of the new men would be able to give their speeches. I started to worry. Speeches and time passed. Then the emcee said, "Sorry, we have to stop there. Our time is up."

Mike and I looked at each other in disbelief. What? Not even a chance to win the big, blue box? We were steamed. While we fumed, the emcee announced that the judges had chosen two speakers to participate in a runoff. They would have to give extemporaneous speeches. When their names were announced, I just got madder. Neither of their speeches had struck me as anything but ordinary.

What happened next is a bit foggy, but I do recall that one of the fellows drew the topic "mad dogs and Englishmen go out in the midday sun." Whatever he might have brilliantly concocted to fit in with that theme was lost on me—I was still angry that I hadn't had a chance. My seatmate, I'm sure, was feeling the same. The generalization that males of Irish decent have volatile tempers would have found two examples, side-by-side, to support it.

Okay, so blah, blah, blah, the two finalists duked it out and one was declared a winner. Big cheers. Clapping. I'm sure that I stopped sulking long enough to watch the opening of the box. The emcee led the cheers as the winner exposed his prize: It was a toilet seat.

The stunned winner was asked to hold up his prize. Even from a distance of about thirty feet, I could see names, presumably of past winners, painted on the seat. At St. John's, in deference to the seminary's namesake, the toilets were not called "johns." One spoke, instead, of going to the "jakes," the nicknamed version of John. The Gaudete Sunday Speech Contest winner, a lad named Gerald Daly, was the 1961 winner of the "Jakes Memorial Award." On close inspection, one could see that his name was already on the award.

The fix had been in all along. Gerald Daly, I was shortly told, won because he was the first to sign up as a member of the "new men" of 1961. As all the assembled seminarians went to the basement of prep side to the area where cold drinks and candy bars were to be had, which, that night, were "on the house," Mike and I went down together. He hadn't grasped that we had been bamboozled. He wanted to know where the real prize was and how Daly's name came to be already on the "prize." On the way to the basement, it was Don Barker, an old friend of mine who was in sixth prep who explained to me that Daly's seniority among the new men had been the criterion for picking him as the winner. He also told me that Mike and I were left off the speakers' list just as part of the whole hoax—that the chief pranksters probably suspected that we were keen to compete. So in this night of devious deception, we played an unknowing role in the trickery. He also pointed out what I hadn't noticed: that Bishop Fletcher never showed up.

It took me a while to convince Mike that the whole thing was sham. His earnest belief in the institution of the Gaudete Sunday Speech Contest wasn't easily shaken. "It was all a hoax! A trick! We were duped!" I told him. When he finally accepted it, I could tell that it was going to take a while for him to appreciate the silence and the skullduggery and the deception that it took, over many weeks, to make the Jakes Memorial Award tradition so successful. We could now count ourselves as joining the conspirators when the next year's Gaudete special night was announced.

*

A fellow prep-sider approached me. He asked me if I could do him a favor. His mother happened to live in Little Rock, and he asked me if I could, that night, drive a car that he had already arranged to borrow from one of the faculty to take him and his mother to the train station. It took him a while to make me understand that she wasn't the only one travelling; he was leaving the seminary. I said I would, but before he finalized things with me about when we'd be going, he wanted to make the circumstances of their leaving clear to me. "My father has threatened to kill my mother, so that's why we're leaving."

That added a dimension to an extraordinary request that made it even more extraordinary. I could see in his face the concern and perhaps even fear that marked his dropping out of the seminary. Having heard the extenuating circumstances, I honored my agreement to drive. In a way I was glad that it would be within a few hours, and not a day or two away—less time to lose my nerve.

The train was supposed to leave late, around 10:00. His mother had vacated the family home after her husband's threat, and we picked her up about an hour before departure at the house of a friend. I blamed my mother for the tension that I experienced in the next sixty minutes. She had taught me that when one took another to a train station or an airport, good manners required that one waited until the person's actual departure from the station or gate took place before leaving oneself. So I was stuck.

As the three of us sat on a long, pew-like bench, my classmate had his eyes riveted on the main door to the station. I took his cue and watched as well, both of us looking for his father, even though I didn't know what he looked like. To say the "minutes dragged," as one commonly does in tense circumstances, is to understate their second-by-second lack of forward progress. The announcement that their train was boarding evoked three sighs, and he and she, each carrying one suitcase, left Little Rock. I got back to St. John's after lights-out, and everybody seemed to know that he was gone, that I had played a part in his exit, yet no one ever asked me to explain any of the details. My guess was that the priest who lent me his car had spoken to the others in fifth prep and told them what he wanted them to know and that they should make no further inquiries of him or me.

*

One of our fifth prep members, a guy from Orlando, Florida, was a fan of flatulence. You may have had the misfortune to know the type. He introduced the subject as often as he was able and found much hilarity in it. One of his favorite times to do so was after we had retired for the night but before many of us had fallen asleep. He didn't stay long at St. John's, and, speaking for myself only, I wasn't sorry to see him and his brand of humor leave.

One night after his departure from St. John's, with all of us in our bunks and sleep approaching, grand silence was broken, not by anyone speaking but by a plane that broke the sound barrier. Mike O'Malley immediately quipped, "All the way from Orlando." The general outburst of laughter was too great for senior man Ray Linder to cite Mike for a grand silence violation. It was the best one-liner I heard in four years at the sem.

*

Sports were big at St. John's. Whether because of their ability to distract us from rigorous study or act as outlets for pent-up emotions, the various athletic activities involved almost everyone, even those not much inclined to them. We had leagues identified as "A" and "B," with the latter for those not especially gifted or interested in sports. Touch and later flag football were the order of the day in the fall, and basketball and softball came when the time of year called for them.

Both prep side and the upper side had their own football fields, and Ray Linder, the aforementioned senior man of our class, was involved in play that sticks in my mind. Ray's team was on defense; the other team was about to score. But the quarterback threw a pass that Ray intercepted in his own end zone. I don't know if Ray knew that he could have stopped in the end zone and his team would have been given the ball on the twenty-yard line. In any case, he decided to run the ball out of the end zone. Ray was long-legged and soon he was ahead of all the other team's players. Ray didn't stop running until he reached his own end zone. If our prep side field wasn't exactly the regulation 100 yards long, it was close to it.

When Ray got to the end zone, he didn't spike the ball or toss it in the air. He fell on it. And when we who were either trying to chase him down or block for him caught up to him, prostrate, he didn't look good. His face was flushed, and he seemed to be on the verge of losing consciousness. A grave situation, I thought. Some guys huddled around him while others were shouting, "Give him air!" Thankfully in a minute or two he sat up and quickly recovered. As I said, the incident has remained with me for over fifty years. And when I saw and talked to Ray just a couple of months ago, the first time we have laid eyes on each other in five decades, he didn't remember anything about it!

*

The majority of boys and men who were studying at St. John's were from Arkansas, but the fellows from other dioceses were close behind in terms of numbers. This nearly equal division explained why the tradition of the Arkies, at the end of the football season, playing one last game against all comers, came into existence, long before I ever arrived. It was the "Home-Foreign" game, and we on prep side had our game, and the men on the upper side had theirs. Ours was played in the morning of a Saturday in late November, and the upper side held its game that afternoon.

I think it was 7-man (or boy) football: three blockers, three receivers, and a quarterback. I was to be the passer for our Home team, and we had in fifth and sixth prep several good players to be the pass-catchers, but we were lacking any stout lads to be the blockers. The defense could rush only three players, so on each play it was our quarterback protectors against their hard-charging rushers. When I asked if the boys who were in high school could play in the game, I was told that they were eligible, but they hardly ever had the talent to play against boys who were college freshmen or sophomores.

I suggested we enlist four of the high school boys, all pretty good sized, and see if they could do the job. Skepticism about their youth was the main reason for my proposal to be met lukewarmly. But finally I was able to get them a tryout, and they did well enough that eventually, for lack of good-sized collegians, they became the offensive line.

The game was touch football as far as stopping the forward progress of the ball carrier was concerned, but the blocking to protect the passer and the rushing to try to get to him involved significant bodily contact between the two lines. Nobody had any protective padding on. Our linemen (or lineboys) had to block with their hands pinned to their chests, elbows extended, while those rushing could use their hands to push and shove, though not grab the blockers.

Our four young linemen rotated in and out of the game to give one a rest while the others tried to hold off the defense. By the game's end, I was the hero, not for any great playing, even though we won, but for thinking of using the "kids." They played great against players as many as five years older than they were. I will take credit, however, for a trick play that worked to perfection. It was called "three men off, two men on."

This low-down ploy was legal, though perhaps not as ethical as one would expect to see in a game involving seminarians. Before the game started, I had alerted the officials of our intent to run the play. As they were all from the upper side, I trusted that none of them, even if "foreign," would squeal on us. None did.

On the play, we sent three men to the sideline, ostensibly to be replaced by three substitutes, but only two subs ran on the field. One of the three who had seemingly left the field of play stood just barely in bounds at the sideline. Our real subs, on their side of the sideline, were to stand right next to him, making it appear that he was off the field. Thus, he was flanked out at least twenty-five yards from where the next snap was to take place.

When I threw the ball to him, he was totally unguarded. On defense, L.D. (the noisy snoozer/bottle tosser) was heard to shout, "What the hell?" as our split end caught the ball and ran for a touchdown. That was a lot of fun, as it was to win the game.

That afternoon, we "home" and "foreign" boys from prep side went to the upper side field to witness the men's version of Home-Foreign. And it was quite a different version! The blocking was ferocious. The rushers were coming full tilt at the quarterback and the sound of body collision on every play was shocking compared to our much milder version. Some of the players were in their mid-twenties and had achieved full growth, making the conflict between the two lines almost scary.

I don't recall the outcome of the game, but I do remember one comment I heard after it. One of the Arkansas players was Dale Castro, a rangy, tall, strong young man who was a lineman in for virtually every play. I noticed that he and his opposite number clashed violently on every play. As Dale left the field, exhausted and probably very sore, he said, "Man, if I had known it was going to be this rough, I'd have worn a jock!"

*

I made a crack earlier that implied the food at St. John's was bad. I also mentioned that the building wherein it was served was called the refectory. It was nicked named the "He knows faith" building, too. When I first heard that name, I asked about it. I was provided with the Latin noun and verb that are translated "he knows faith": *fidem scit*. I will leave it to you to figure out the church Latin pronunciation of those two words.

Only three Olivitan Benedictine nuns prepared meals for about 160 of us a day. Their hard, unceasing work no doubt landed each in a pinnacle in heaven, and the gripes about the food had nothing to do with their culinary skills. It was about the amount of money they had to spend to purchase the food. Once a delegation of upper siders went to the seminary's boss with complaints about the food. They were surprised when their question about the allotment of money per day for food was answered: less than two dollars! In any case, the food was bad because the greatest chef in the world could not have done better than our three nuns.

The least bad meal of the day was breakfast, because it was mainly two things: cereal and toast. The cereal came in those little, one-person serving boxes. Sometimes one could find a particular kind one liked. I even came to downing Kix with some regularity, a brand I never ate as a civilian. Fixing perhaps 300 pieces of toast each morning must have been a tough assignment. I saw, when on kitchen duty to wash dishes, that the bread was browned in the oven on large cookie sheets. Obviously there was no way to keep it warm when the time came to eat it. In winter months, though, seminarian ingenuity found a way to heat it up. Radiators! On chilly mornings one could see balanced on those steam-powered warming devices that lined at least one wall of "He knows faith," dozens of pieces of toast, acquiring something of that just-out-of-the-toaster quality. I noticed that a protein-obtaining process was at work at breakfast among many of my fellows: putting peanut butter on their toast. Each table had a jar of peanut butter, but not a brand with which I was familiar. For someone reared on Peter Pan, any other marque was foreign, especially Shedd's, which was the only one in evidence at St. John's. I ate it a few times and found it harmless, but my speculation is that Shedd's (now obsolete) was a bargain compared to P.P.P.B.

One morning in late fall or early winter, I was in for a shock when I entered the refectory for breakfast. He didn't know faith on that day! The smell of bacon, unmistakable, uplifting, enticing, and my favorite breakfast ingredient, was clearly in the air! What was going on? An old hand said, "It's the Deacon Breakfast." I wrote that name with capital letters because it was so welcome to my olfactory and, ultimately, my gustatory senses. Once again the lads who were not in their first year had kept a secret from us new guys. Was there some kind of vow that one took at the end of his first year at the sem that bound one to silence about things deemed secret? Whatever process was used to create tight lips was extraordinarily effective.

The once-a-year project called for the deacon class, which is to say the men in their last year at the seminary and who would be ordained as priests the following spring, not only to pay for the bacon but to fry it. So they must have been up at least an hour before the rest of us (who rose at 6:00), diligently tending to pans and grease and whatever else was required to provide enough slices for about thirteen dozen of us to break their fasts with the salty, aromatic delight.

I ate twelve pieces.

*

In case you're wondering about the religious aspects of the seminary, I present for your consideration our Sunday schedule (key details provided by Al Schneider), all of which took place in the main chapel on the upper side but for the last two:

6:30 a.m. to 7:30 –	Meditation and low Mass (one without singing)
10:30 to11:45 –	High Mass (yes, with singing— and a sermon)
11:55 to noon –	Angelus
4:30 to 5:00 –	Vespers (the evening prayer of the church) and Benediction
5:30 to 6:00 –	Rosary
9:30 -9:45 –	Compline (end-of-the-day prayer)

My memory of Sundays is that they required mental preparation to endure without prayer and chapel fatigue setting in. The Sunday High Mass was our one chance per week to sport the biretta, the black "beanie" as some called it, and we were taught that there was only one right way to wear it. The three prongs on top were key to the correct positioning. The biretta was taken in the right hand with the prongs pointing to the 12:00, 3:00, and 6:00 positions; the one at 3:00 was grasped, and then the cap was placed on the head, with the 3:00 prong more or less above the right ear. Any other position besides the middle prong pointing east was not ecclesiastically kosher.

*

Not one, but two killers showed up at St. John's when I was in fifth prep. The first was in relation to a radio report.

Though radios, other than those in common recreation areas, were outlawed, more than a few of the small, easily hidden transistor type were apparently on campus. Which type was responsible for the news, I don't know. I was told that a man who had been charged with murder was at the state hospital being examined for possible mental problems but had escaped. That hospital must have been at least four or five miles distant from the sem. Later I heard through the grapevine (no transistor in my possession—yet) that he had been spotted somewhere on the "Heights," the neighborhood in which we were located. The news spread all over prep side that police were in the area, searching for him. Ten o'clock and lights-out were approaching. I was coming back to our dorm after brushing my teeth when a boy from sixth prep stepped out of his dorm, which was just across the hall from ours. His face was blackened, perhaps with shoe polish, and in his hand was a hatchet.

Once again there was a ruse afoot. "Where are you going?" I asked, pretty sure I knew where. "To the high school dorm," he replied, a glint in his eye and a big grin on his face. The high school boys were all in one dormitory, and when the "killer" appeared after lights out, only a dim light from the hallway outside the dorm illuminated him. From what I heard the next day, he evoked a lot of screams, shouts, and prayers when he stalked about the room. The kicker in all this is that the two priests who were in charge of prep side lived on that floor and had to be in on the charade for it to take place. If I didn't remind myself to have that grain of salt handy on a daily basis, I should have. St. John's was hell on gullibility.

The other killer looked like an altar boy, which I'm sure he had been. He was maybe five feet tall (on tiptoes), and might have been approaching one hundred pounds (in a year or two). His victims were his fellow seminarians. Most of us on prep side quickly learned to avoid him unless we were deluded enough to imagine we could bring him down. Jim Rossi was this killer's name, and pool was his game. My recollection is that he was from a small, mostly Catholic community called Center Ridge, and though I doubt the town was full of pool halls, there surely had to be one there, because this kid showed up at St. John's with the kind of skill that nowadays coincides with the popular notion that it takes 10,000 hours of practice to develop a physical talent to its fullest.

The cherubic, blond-headed assassin was soft-spoken, polite, and would rip your heart out when a green-felted level surface and sixteen balls were involved. It wasn't long before Rossi's reputation as conqueror of all comers on prep side drifted north, where the upper side was located. He was invited to visit where the big boys played and dispatched them all. His greatest victory in my mind came after clobbering yet another player probably ten years older than he. The loser was kind of grumpy, and Rossi quietly asked if he wanted to take a bet. A bet on what? Rossi wordlessly went to the table's pockets and withdrew six balls. He placed one immediately in front of each of the six pockets. He put the cue ball on a black dot about two feet from the end of the table and proposed a bet that went perhaps as high as a quarter. "I bet you can't sink all the balls on the table in six shots."

The loser looked amused at the simplicity of the task. He said, "You're on!" and quickly went about the business of sinking each of the six balls. "You lose," he chortled. Among those who had been watching the game, there was one who was not only observing; he was listening. "No he didn't. You didn't sink the cue ball! He said, 'Sink all the balls on the table.' You lose."

Much laughter ensued, and the double-loser looked like he was ready to blow, but Rossi smiled, said something about it was "just for fun," and left. I don't know if he ever got another invitation to skin the hides of those on the upper side. Jim Rossi was another example of things at St. John's Seminary not being what they seemed.

*

Those of us new to fifth prep were advised that another tradition awaited us. New students were expected to make a hike from St. John's to Pinnacle Mountain, a hill west of Little Rock. Travel by car is about twelve miles. The route that was used to get there, however, was along railroad tracks. Walking north from St. John's, through woods, eventually led one down a hillside that, at bottom, revealed the tracks that headed west, which could be followed to the mountain in question. On a map the hiking route looks about as long as does the one for drivers.

I learned in Boy Scouts that a walker at a brisk pace could cover a mile in about fifteen minutes. So a dozen miles along rail-road tracks (not an always level surface) would likely take at least three hours. None of us knew at the time either the distance or the time needed to get there, and I don't think anybody asked; heck, it sounded like a fun way to spend some time on Satur-day. As I recall, of the veterans only Al Schneider and Ray Linder accompanied us new guys on the journey. And not all the newcomers were there, though I don't know what excuses were used to get out of the forced march.

What started out as a happy hike became, after an hour or so, a sad slog. The snappy chatter at the outset was replaced by mostly silence or complaints about the shaky footing along the tracks. We neophytes were surprised to see a house not far off the route, a well worn wood abode that had a front-yard faucet visible at the end of a perpendicular pipe that looked to be a couple of feet sticking out of the ground. As we approached the house, an elderly woman emerged into her yard.

The sight of a group of young males didn't cause her to retreat into her home, and when one of our company near the front of our line saw a metal dipper hanging from the faucet, he asked her if we might stop for a drink. She was agreeable, and we lined up to get a swig. Charlie Lipsmeyer, my Catholic High classmate, spoke four words that sent her, looking alarmed, straight inside, words that were innocent but that she obviously didn't interpret that way: "Do you live alone?"

Charlie was mystified that she so clearly felt threatened, and later, after we had gone farther down the tracks, we tried to communicate why his word choice might have upset her. We who hadn't drunk yet from her faucet decided to pass, leaving her front yard ASAP, lest she be further disturbed by our presence.

The eventual arrival at Pinnacle Mountain meant that less than half the day's calorie-burning was complete, because the mountain-like projection itself needed to be scaled for the tradition to be honored. One of us had a camera along, and I have, to this day, a picture of the group of us (minus the cameraman) sprawling atop the hill, looking weary.

The return journey was by means of the highway, which was state highway 10, a much busier route now than then, so the danger of walking single file along its shoulder was not nearly so potentially hazardous as it would be nowadays. The group of us thinned out as we headed home. I recall that three of us were separated the others. One said, "I'm sticking my thumb out as we walk—I'm tired."

Neither the other hiker nor I objected. I'm sure we all knew that hitchhiking wasn't part of the "tradition," but none of us cared about that at the time. The more I think of it, I'm pretty sure we had outpaced the others, because when a truck pulled up and we piled in the bed of it, our arrival back in Little Rock was such that we hung out on Kavanaugh, the main drag in the Heights area that had lots of stores where we could idle away some time. I believe we three made a vow to deny that we had gotten a ride. We wasted some time before getting back to St. John's, not wanting to get back too early before the rest. I think our violation of the spirit of the adventure went unnoticed.

*

Friday nights at St. John's were evenings when school work could be ignored, but the array of down-time diversions were few. You already know we could play pool, but that was fun for only the best players, since the duds among us didn't get much time at the table. Card-playing had its adherents, but that too had a short shelf life for many of us. I recall that one Friday, as a desperate attempt to kill time, I volunteered to give another guy a shave.

We had a couple of barber chairs on prep side; fellow seminarian hair whackers, who had previously been amateurs, would charge a much lower fee for "lowering one's ears" than the local barbers on Kavanaugh. It was at one of these chairs that my Catholic High classmate Jerry Sweetman sat himself, preparing for the first shave he had ever gotten from me, and probably anyone else—and the first I had ever given.

Prior to putting himself in such a perilous spot, Jerry had said, "I've never gotten a good shave." Looking at him, I asked, "What do you mean?" I could see that he had a heavier beard than I was accustomed to scraping in the mornings, but I figured that enough effort could make his face free of any "shadow." So I volunteered to do that, and he accepted.

It was 1961, mind you, and so the modern, multiple-layered bladed razors were still unknown. I used a Gillette Safety razor, a double-edged device probably thrice the weight of modern beard-hackers. In that I installed a new blade, the ultra-sharp Gillette Blue Blade, a shaver's best friend for complete hair removal. Jerry shook the can of foam, applied a pile of it to his hand and then to his face, and leaned back in the barber chair, trustingly—unaware, I'm sure, that he was allowing a complete novice to scrape his face with a sharp instrument.

But it went well—at least as well as not drawing any blood was concerned. When I finished and Jerry rinsed off the residual foam and examined my work, he said, "That's the way it always looks for me, too. But thanks for trying."

"Oh, you thought I was finished!" I quickly replied, determined to get him to say that I had done a stellar job. Emboldened by getting through round one with no injury, I told him I wasn't finished. He got back and submitted to another going-over with a new blade—and then another. The triple whammy to any whiskers. Rinsing, patting his face dry, and then rubbing his hand over his mouche after round three, Jerry said, "You did it! That's the closest shave I ever got. Thanks!"

I was proud. Though I hadn't planned on it taking three spins around the block, we finally arrived at our destination. Perhaps it was only a half-hour later that I saw Jerry again. He was in our dorm, asking if anyone had any kind of lotion that might relieve pain. His face, at least that section where hair that we call a *beard* grows, or grew, was red, a shade that one would associate with a severe sunburn—or a face that has been shaved three times.

Jerry was very understanding, but nodded in agreement after my apology and promise that his was my last shave to give to anyone but myself.

*

Outside the area where the barber chairs were located was the site of the first "Swedish snow bath" that I ever witnessed. The initial snowfall of the school year came late one afternoon and lasted long enough for a couple of inches to accumulate as the evening wore on. Like the night of three shaves, it was Friday. Snowballers (especially those from snow-starved states like Florida) were doing their thing, and as I stepped outside to observe the fun, from out of the corner of my eye I saw a figure running into the area. It was L.D.; you remember him.

Three odd things then occurred before the fourth: first, L.D.'s body seemed to be emitting steam (he had just taken a hot shower, I later learned); second, he was naked (not unusual if one just come from the shower, but odd outside the building); third, he lay flat on his back in the snow, making the familiar snow angel with expanding and contracting leg and arm movements. The fourth odd thing was L.D.'s baptism of the event as he re-entered the building: "That's a Swedish snow bath."

*

Our religion class in fifth prep was taught by a very admirable deacon. He was tall, slender, athletic, modest, friendly, and spiritual young man. He drove us nuts.

Deacon Tim stood before us in our daily class and spoke clearly, in a pleasant voice, avoiding the typical *you knows* and *uhs* that punctuate the speech of so many of us. But still, when he addressed us, it was difficult to follow what he was saying...make that *impossible*. The problem was one of which I'm sure he was unaware, and none of us had the temerity, or chutzpah, or guts, or whatever it would have taken, to tell him.

From the center of his upper lip to his lower, a thin string of spittle would form as he talked. And then, rubber-band-like, it went up and down as the words he chose either caused his lips to part or to close. It wasn't unbreakable. It would separate, seem to disappear, and then re-appear. On occasion, he would lick his lips and it would also vanish, but it never left for long.

The coping mechanisms for his auditors were varied: Some counted the number of times the band would rise and fall before breaking; others would silently count "one Mississippi, two Mississippi" to determine the length of seconds between appearance and disappearance; others said they counted the number of words uttered between creation and demise of the band. We worried that when he became a priest he would similarly drive his congregation batty with the trait. We comforted ourselves that, as one of my classmates put it, "Some kid will tell him even if no adult will." We hoped so. He was a nice guy.

*

Don Barker was my early boyhood pal (and remained one despite the fact that in a basketball game, and on opposing teams, I took advantage of the fact that we had played together for years, so that when I called, "Don!" he threw me the ball.) Don's sense of humor was one which I will politely describe as *quirky*. As I mentioned earlier, he was a year ahead of me at St. John's. One day when it was raining, Don went to the aid of someone who was without an umbrella. Don gave him his umbrella. This fellow was standing alongside the refectory as the rain came down, staying dry thanks to Don. Few other than Don would have thought to put an umbrella in the right hand of the statue of Jesus.

Though Don had moved with his family to Texas when he was in high school, he was at St. John's studying for the diocese of Little Rock. That is how he came to be one of the players for the Home team when it came time for the football game against the Foreign team. You already know the outcome of that game, but I held out until now to describe the Barker Pass Play. We practiced a couple of afternoons for the "big game," and at one practice Don proposed a pass pattern for two of our receivers that he said came from the world of square dancing. I can't vouch for the accuracy of the name he eventually gave to it, but when I describe what it involved, I think you'll recognize the maneuver.

Don got two pass catchers to line up on opposite ends of what would have been the line of scrimmage. He instructed them to both run forward about five steps and then cut to the middle, virtually running straight at each other. As they were about to collide, the receiver coming from the right was to extend his right arm, as if escorting a woman on his arm, and the receiver from the left was to do the same.

If you have been able to follow my description, you know what happened next: They entwined their arms, swung around in a half-circle and headed back in the direction from which they came. Don promised it would baffle their defenders and leave each receiver open to catch a pass.

"That's the do-si-do," Don proudly announced to much laughter when two players successfully ran their pass routes. Come Saturday, and we're in the midst of our only important game of the year, and I'm in the huddle about to call a play (something complicated like "Andy, you go down and out 10 yards," and "Mark, you go long"). That's when Don said, "Hey, Mo, time for the do-si-do?" Again the laughter. I could see in his face that Don was serious. "Sure, let's run it." As he predicted, both receivers were open, and I threw it for a good gain to You-Know-Who.

*

I think that in high school I smoked one cigarette. It was disgusting! At St. John's the smokers were many. Consumption of tobacco was widespread. I think even the high school boys could smoke. Cigarette smokers outnumbered the pipe fellows by a wide margin, but the minority pipe puffers made a sort of sacrament out of their hobby/habit, and spent an inordinate amount of time, I thought, discussing their combinations of tobacco and the types of pipes they favored.

The favorite brand of cigarettes among fifth preppers was Lucky Strike. I believe this was an era where Lucky Strike had no filtered version of itself, so it was just tobacco, paper, a little glue, and maybe a thousand chemicals that composed its contents. It was clear from my first days that some of my classmates were not new to smoking and that others were tyros. I soon joined the latter group, struggling to overcome my body's natural inclination to reject the inhalation of the burning ingredients I just mentioned. But I soldiered on, and eventually was "hooked," as we were wont to say. It is a tribute to St. John's, its faculty, its students, and its traditions to say that my smoking is the only thing about my experience there that I regret. I was eighteen when I began to smoke, and I did not stop until 39 years later, and it was unfiltered Luckies that I inhaled from start to finish. I'm hoping that my 16 years of not indulging have somewhat reversed the effects, but one who smoked for that long can never be sure.

The coterie of pipe smokers engaged in a crusade: to discover the "Royal Mixture," as I heard it described. The "Royal" was to be that blend of various brands and other additives (e.g., apples, cinnamon) in just the right amounts that would be agreed upon as the last word in pipe tobacco. Each member of the group was welcome to try to come up with the formula that would deserve to be called Royal, and I heard one day that it had been found.

Fred Webert, perhaps in his deacon year at St. John's, apparently created a combination that satisfied the group's members that he had reached the pinnacle. There was a downside to the discovery, however. Was it that the joy of the hunt had come to an end? No. Fred couldn't remember the ingredients.

*

I mentioned that when we had free time, some boys found cards a welcome diversion. The only card game I have ever really enjoyed is poker—when I'm winning. In the 1950's the game Canasta became extremely popular, and my mother taught it to me, and even though it was played with multiple decks and was unlike any other game of cards I had ever played, somehow I never contracted Canasta fever.

One of the priests on the St. John's faculty was Father Anthony Benz, known as "Doc" to his fellow priests (and so-called, but not to his face, by seminarians). Since he and I have spoken by phone on occasion since our days at St. John's and he identifies himself as "Doc," I'll call him that, too.

Doc Benz was a pinochle player. And he was always on the hunt to find new players (though *victims* would be a more apt word) Few seminarians knew how to play pinochle, so he had to be an instructor before he could become an opponent. He was a very patient teacher—pinochle has its complications. I witnessed him tutoring would-be pinochlers and admired his willingness to help even the most knuckle-headed of beginners, a group that eventually included me. As you may have gathered, Doc was far too good at pinochle for his opponents. And I never thought that winning was his primary goal. He just loved to play, and he exulted when the opposing team beat his, letting everybody nearby know what the lads had done.

My career as an opponent of Doc's was short. Being one of those annoying competitive types, I'm not one who is, for long, going to play a game at which his chances of winning are slim. So with that in mind you will understand (though probably not sympathize with) my reason for getting off the pinochle circuit. I and a teammate, without hope of success, were taking on Doc and his partner. At a point not especially far into the game, Doc announced that the game was over. I'm sure this wasn't bragging on his part. He just wanted to start another game, one that might be more competitive. "How do you know you've won?" asked my teammate, a lad without enough experience to be able to hear the fat lady singing. The doubting fellow then turned incredulous when Doc said, "I know what you have in your hands." The questioner didn't notice the plural *hands*. The boy asked Doc to say what cards he held, and Doc told him. He looked disbelievingly at his cards. "What about the other guys?" Doc told him, and we showed our cards. All were what he predicted. How he did it, I couldn't say, but after another game or two, with identical outcomes, my pinochle career came to a close.

*

pre-1961: At some point in its history, St. John's became an outpost for St. Louis University's seismograph placement program. In the basement of the refectory were instruments to record any unusual seismic events, up to and including earthquakes. I tagged along once when one of the seminarians whose job it was to service the machinery carried out his duty. I remember that a cylinder of a couple feet in length and with a diameter of possibly a foot was feeding a long roll of paper to another like-sized cylinder. A long, skinny pointer that had ink at its tip traveled lightly across the page to measure the movement of terra firma (or unfirma). The long rolls, I was told, were occasionally replaced with others, and the inky ones were sent to Missouri. I link the seismograph to an event that took place a year or two before my arrival.

I don't know what percentage of seminarians even knew of the seismograph, but I wouldn't be surprised if its presence on the campus might have influenced those who did know of it to interpret what happened one night after lights out as an earthquake. It was, however, apparently just old age that caused a ceiling to fall in. And it was the ceiling that ran at least half the length of the floor where the fifth and sixth prep dorms were located. The falling plaster blocked the exit from the dorms, sent up a cloud of dust enough to strangle a camel, and terrified the boys in the high school dorm, one of whom, according to legend, ran so fast out the front door on the second floor that he failed to slow down enough to take the steps that led to the first level. Somehow he survived his daredevil escape. Others, stuck in their sixth prep dorm by the debris blocking their door and then thinking the dust was smoke and that the building was on fire, tied sheets together and threw them out the windows (after tying them off on something stable) to use as an escape route.

I bet that someone later checked to see if the seismograph registered any unusual activity before—or as—the ceiling came down.

*

One fifth prepper, call him Emcee, was older than the rest of us, by how many years I couldn't guess then, and still can't.

Just older. OK, if you have to have a number, I'd say seven-and-a-half years. Being clearly our senior, he acted like it, dispensing information and suggestions when requested, and also when not. I thought he was recruiting acolytes, in the secular sense of the term. I think he knew I wasn't a good candidate to be a follower, but one day, out of nowhere he announced, "I could hypnotize you." I told him I probably wasn't a good candidate, being too weak-minded to be influenced, but he persisted. Finally, I agreed to let him try. We got together in some room free of distractions and others, maybe the auditorium, and I was uneasy about that. Being alone with him was kind of creepy. We sat in folding chairs, too close for comfort in my view, and he pulled out a pocket watch and chain, the standard tools of the hypnotist.

He began to wave the watch before my eyes and told me, his breath kind of skunky, that I was getting sleepy. What I was, was bored. He told me I was becoming acutely sleepy and instructed me to close my eyes and to continue to imagine the swaying timepiece. He then told me that when he snapped his fingers I could open my eyes, but not until. Then, in a soft but commanding voice he said, "The next time that you see your friend Charlie Lipsmeyer, no matter where he is, you will walk up to him and sock him in the right shoulder. You will not remember anything that I have said when you awaken." I heard his fingers snap and opened my eyes. We got up from where we had been sitting and walked without comment back to our dorm. Inside, talking to two guys, was Charlie. I knew Emcee was right behind me. I strode alongside Charlie, raised my arm as one would before delivering a punch, then walked away. Emcee didn't have much to do with me after that. And that wasn't a bad thing, because he was asked to leave the seminary not long after.

Emcee's departure had to do with an extraordinary gathering in the main chapel of all twelve years' worth of us seminarians. Monsignor O'Connell, the rector, had called us together to speak. His message was strange; it had to do with his role should extraordinary things be happening to us, such as seeing visions or hearing talking birds. Should we find ourselves confronted with such things, he told us that we should check with him to determine their source or veracity. The point of the speech was lost on all of us who communed about it afterwards. It turned out that Monsignor O'Connell was trying to communicate with a group about whom he knew little except that it existed somewhere at St. John's. I later was told that some seminarians were gathering in out-of-the-way places in the wee hours to discuss a new form of religion and to consult with beings that were located in the great beyond. Apparently my would-be spell-caster Emcee was the chief instigator, and when he and others didn't step forward and identify themselves to the rector, when he did eventually find out who they were, he gave them their walking papers. It wouldn't be the last time when we would hear a veiled message in that chapel.

*

One of the guys in fifth prep was not exactly my idea of what a pre-priest was like. To say he was unfriendly is fair; to say he was surly is also probably accurate. So when I heard him speaking to another fellow about one of the seminarians who had just been kicked out, I was surprised when he said, "I hated to see him go." Wow! Was I mistaken; this guy really wasn't as anti-social as I thought. Then I heard his second sentence about the recently departed: "He had the best damn pipe-reamer in the whole seminary."

*

The big sporting event in winter was known as "The Inter-House Series," a basketball tournament. The contests pitted against each other the three groups that constituted the seminary: Prep Side, Philosophers, and Theologians. We prep siders were, as I mentioned, the high school boys and the first two years of college. The Philosophers, who lived on the upper side, were the last two college years. The Theologians consisted of the men in their last four years. The schedule called for us to play the Philosophers on Friday, and the winner (invariably the Philosophers) to play the Theologians for the championship the next night.

We had a "coach," a deacon, and I suggest with the quotation marks that I'm using the term lightly because I don't recall that he coached us, except that he sat on our bench the night we played the Philosophers. Counting yours truly, we had three Irish guys in the lineup, and Mike Ryan and Pat Donovan were, as now we often hear said of accomplished players, "ballers."

Ryan was short, fast, and could shoot a long-range shot (before it was worth three points) with deadly accuracy. Donovan was tall, strong, and could rebound with the best of 'em. When we beat the Philosophers on Friday, true amazement among our fans abounded. St. John's gym was so small that my mention of a *bench* was exaggerated. Folding chairs placed at an angle to lessen their exposure to the court made up the bench. It was standing room only for any but the few subs that each team had. The number of spectators who showed up for the game surprised me, though in retrospect I realize that there wasn't much else to do on Friday except take the short walk to the gym. *Everybody* was there! And I played in some gyms that were full and loud, but I never heard anything like the uproar that I heard that night. The gym was so small and the fans so vociferous that when they got heated up, hearing anything distinct was impossible.

I have a vivid memory of seeing one of our high school boys on the sideline, screaming with delight as we pulled away from the Philosophers with time expiring. That he was simultaneously using a baseball bat to pound on a garbage can was but a part of the ear-pounding din. Defeating the older guys was an upset so unlikely that nobody who was on prep side, even those in their sixth year there, could remember it ever happening. In a matter of an hour, the time it took for the game to begin and end, basketball fever gripped prep side.

The next day, as the night's showdown with the Theologians loomed, the talk was of little else other than "What if...?" The excitement among the prep siders was great fun to see and hear, especially that among the high school boys, one of whose number, Mike Adams, was among our key players. Mike was only a freshman, but one who was bound to be a very tall adult, as he was second in height only to Donovan and was already a good player.

When we beat the Theologians later that evening, our deacon "coach" said it had "never been done," though I'm sure he was speaking of only during his own time at the sem, not in the entire history of the series. But nit-picking the claim aside, it was a joyous evening for us, the junior members of the community, and the few dozen of us who made up the prep side gathered in a group to walk to the upper side and serenade them with a song, one that I'm sure was appropriate to the occasion, maybe something along the lines of "Good night, losers—good night, losers—good night, losers, we hate to see you go!"

*

One priest was the spiritual director for the whole seminary. He lived on the upper side, and while visiting a friend there, I, for the first time, passed his room on the top floor. From that room came the sound of music. Ignorant for the most part about music of any kind besides rock and roll and the pop music my sisters listened to in the 1950's, the best I could do to identify it was to think of the broad term *classical*. Once back on prep side I mentioned what I had heard to an old hand, and he told me that it was, instead, *opera*, and that our spiritual director listened to no other type. I immediately classified him as a very cultured fellow, no doubt sophisticated and brainy. I knew that he looked the part, as I had seen him walking on campus in a flowing black cassock, tinged here and there with red, the outfit of a monsignor.

We who were in the minor seminary, as opposed to those on the major, or upper side, didn't have much contact with him. Apparently his main concern was with the older seminarians. But in the spring, we first-year seminarians on prep side got the word one evening that we were to go to the main chapel, because the spiritual director was going to address us. Our veteran brothers looked amused at the appointment that we newcomers were to keep, but they were tight-lipped, as usual, about the occasion. The C.I.A. should have inquired at St. John's about how the seminary created walls of silence that no one ever seemed to break. It was an annoying thing to be once again in the circumstance of experiencing a tradition about which no one would spill the beans!

And so went, at the designated time, all of us newcomers from prep side, ranging in age from fourteen to twenty. When we got to the chapel, we saw a few upper siders there as well— of course, there were some new guys there, too. We newbies were there, but where was he, the man of the hour? We either sat or knelt for a few minutes, long enough for me to wonder if the gathering was just another hoax. But then he entered the chapel, from the vestibule, as we had done. He walked from the back of the church to the area of the altar, his monsignor's robes flowing as he strode, elegantly it seemed. I think he was wearing a biretta. If so, his appearance would have been even more impressive. We stood, as one would if a priest had come into the chapel to say Mass. He ascended three steps to the level on which the altar stood and went to a bench at the side. If he had on a biretta, that would have been where he doffed it and would have placed it on the bench. He then bent over a bit and activated what I then saw for the first time: a tape recorder. For whom the tape was intended, I couldn't guess, but the fact that what we were about to hear was being preserved lent even more significance to the occasion.

He turned, faced us, and smiled—a handsome, grey-haired gentleman—motioning to us with both hands that we should be seated. His voice was mellifluous; his words flowed; he spoke for perhaps ten minutes. When finished, he strode again past us and out the chapel. Then we left, too. As we walked back to prep side, one question from our group summed up what was the general reaction to what we had just heard: "What the hell was that all about?"

He had spoken about the coming summer, when we would be home, our first year in the seminary having concluded. At that point, his comments turned to health matters. He said that it was possible that any one of us might experience the onset of one or more boils. He told us that it wouldn't be unusual if that happened. I thought, "I've never had a boil."

Above all, he cautioned, one should never try to open a boil. To do so could endanger one's health. It would inevitably have negative consequences: infection, fever, perhaps even worse results that could prevent one from returning to the seminary. As do all speakers who know how make a point, he reiterated. Don't scratch or otherwise tamper with the boil; leave it alone. It will open naturally on its own, and that will be the best outcome possible. That's when he left, and then we left—puzzled, to say the least.

As we came back to the dorm, we were met with know-ing, enigmatic smiles on the faces of the old boys who had stayed behind. "So what did he talk about?" they asked. We knew that they knew what he talked about, so the same question that was uttered as we left was re-asked.

The explanation came out in miniscule bits, the veterans wanting to eliminate the confusion as grudgingly as possible— verbal water-torture. Finally, one among us who wanted to know "what the hell" it was all about summed up the particles of explanation: "So that was all about masturbation?" Apparently it was.

*

Every other Saturday we were allowed to go off-campus to "the neighborhood," the area called *the Heights* by the local citizenry. One of the buildings there was the Heights Theater, which on Saturday afternoons generally showed kids' movies, and didn't draw a lot of seminarians beyond high school age. Hall's Drug Store was a stopping-off point for any of the items you'd expect in a 1960's store of its ilk. Boshears Cleaners was also on the to-frequent list because of its ability to clean cassocks and wash and iron surplices, as well as satisfying any other dry cleaning needs. But the star attraction in the neighborhood was Browning's Mexican Restaurant. Located about six or seven blocks from St. John's, Browning's was the scene of a line of males, all wearing black slacks and sport shirts, making their way in and out of the eatery from eleven in the morning and for the next five hours.

I have stated a couple of times that the cuisine at St. John's had few fans, so the Tex-Mex offerings at Browning's (plus some American dishes—burgers and superb fried chicken among them) were in great demand. Anyone entering the restaurant on Saturday afternoon who wasn't familiar with the regular weekend influx of seminarians would have been more than a little puzzled at the number of similarly dressed, all-male diners. The no-alcohol-while-enrolled-at-the-seminary rule was sometimes flaunted by daring fellows and conspiratorial waitresses, the occasional beer being poured away from the table into a tall, red, plastic glass usually reserved for fruit punch.

I'm guessing the owners of Browning's, using the law of Arkansas's averages as a basis, were most likely Baptists, but I'm sure they more than once expressed a nighttime prayer of thanks for the nearby Catholic institution, and felt painfully the loss of the black-pants brigade when the seminary closed in 1967.

*

While food is on my mind, I think of the kitchen at St. John's and its inevitable accompaniment, the dish-washing section. We who were the eaters were also the washers. The main job of getting all our plates and silverware clean was accomplished by a seminarian with a hose-like device with a sprayer on its end, which he used to rinse a collection of plates, glasses, and utensils which had been herded into in a hard plastic tray that was then sent on a conveyer-like contraption that carried it all through a washer that generated lots of hot water and steam. It was a hot job that befell one only occasionally, given the large number of seminarians. It might have been a chore that was shared by the upper siders, though I wouldn't be surprised if I have forgotten that it was just the younger set that did the duty. One of the three nuns who worked in the kitchen was typically on hand to extract the tray of just-washed dishes for their next stop, which was a place for them to air dry. The nun who usually carried out that function was a really young woman, not more than 20, I bet. She was friendly but not chatty and did her work efficiently.

I guess we should have seen it coming, but I for one and some others, too, admitted that they didn't either. When one of my fellows from fifth prep started volunteering to take other guys' dishwashing duty, we were too dense (and happy to be rid of the obligation) to realize that his explanation, "I just enjoy doing it," was blarney. When he left the seminary later in the year, and then we heard that the young nun had left shortly thereafter, we finally saw the 1+1 numbers and figured out the connection. I wish I could relate that they both lived happily (and together) ever after, but I don't know what happened next.

*

Fifty-plus years after Mike O'Malley and I entered St. John's, we are still friends. It was there that we really got to know one another, including, as you shall see, rooming together for a year. What I am about to relate is a story that, unfortunately, reinforces stereotypes about Irishmen, that they are hard- and knuckle-headed. I admit that it was I who started it. Some child-hood impulse caused me, while walking past him in our dorm one Friday evening, to tap him lightly on the shoulder, and say, "Got ya last." I put the blame, however, for all that occurred thereafter, on him, since a mature young man would have laughed off the goofy assertion and stayed seated on his bunk. But, no, he had to get up and come after me. I had exited the dorm and was walking down the hall when I realized he was following me. I went quickly down a half-flight of steps and left the building. He did, too. I began to jog, as did he. Then I began to run. "OK, Mal," I thought, "you can stop now." I had increased the space between us. That's when he started to sprint. He was all churning elbows and fierce determination. Amazed, I paused too long, and then he was on me, slapping me on the leg and exulting, "Got ya last!" as he sped by. I had no choice, did I? I was compelled to follow. It was getting dark, but we could still see well enough to run full tilt, without endangering ourselves as we ran through a stand of pines next to the refectory. Though we were both only eighteen and still in pretty good shape, we eventually tired, but he a little sooner than I. Standing, hands on knees, struggling for breath, he was an easy target, as I returned the favor of a tag. Not long after, it was I who was gassed, and he ran me down. Back and forth we went. He was "it," then I. It went on—and on. And, no, I don't remember who got whom "last." We have spoken a few times in five decades about this chase, perhaps both a bit embarrassed by it, given its origin, objective, and length. We agree that the contest may have lasted as long as twenty-five to thirty minutes. We blame it on the Irish in us.

*

Two priests lived on the top floor of our building, Father Walter Clancy, who was in charge of prep side, and Father Everett Ballmann, second in command. They were two very smart, impressive, admirable men, both as teachers and as leaders of the group of young men and boys who lived under their supervision. Father Ballmann was a biblical scholar, versed in multiple languages besides English. His method of corralling the free spirits of those of us who occasionally vented them was the indirect, velvet-glove method. And there was no steel fist within the glove.

One day something went haywire in our dorm, and the volume of voices was far beyond anything that would be considered acceptable indoors. Whether we were cheering or screaming I don't know, but Father Ballmann was passing by (or heard our vociferations from two stories above) and decided to intervene. Had it been I who was there to extinguish the unacceptable noise, I'm sure I would have endeavored to outshout the shouters. "YOU GUYS NEED TO SHUT UP!" Something like that.

Father Ballmann, very low-key and clever, just walked into the dorm and stood there until everyone realized he was there—and shut up. *Gents* was Father Ballmann's word that he used on all occasions to address us. Thus, "Gents, does anybody have a Greek dictionary?" We weren't taking Greek yet, so we all shook our heads. "OK, well, thank you," he said as he exited to total silence. As I said, "low-key and clever."

*

On the last night of the school year, things on prep side got kind of crazy. I recall airborne water balloons, and running in the halls—either in pursuit of or scrambling away from someone who had either thrown such or was the target of one. Some hollering was involved, and more than once we asked and wondered, "Where is Clancy?" Our prep side boss was notably absent from the scene of a kind of chaos that was like only that of the post-Inter-House Series win in its volume. When our enthusiasm for mayhem was just beginning to ebb, down from the top floor strode "Clancy" himself. He was a good-sized man, maybe 6'2", and when he got to the hallway where all the water and spent balloons were visible, every one of us who were unfortunate enough to be in the hallway when he showed up, looming over us, seemed to be the object of his wrath. He bawled us out in no uncertain terms and told us to "clean up and quiet down!"

Though we all felt responsible, it was Tom Kelly, the senior man of sixth prep and thus of prep side as a whole, who stood immediately in front of Father Clancy and took the direct heat for our misbehavior. When Father Clancy ascended the stairs, I was surprised that Tom turned to me and the other miscreants, a smile on his face and a twinkle in his eye, and said, "He's not really mad."

Fooled me! I'd never seen the usually genial priest in a state of mind like that I had just witnessed. Someone asked Tom how he arrived at that unexpected conclusion. "When he's mad, his upper lip quivers when he talks, and there was no quivering. He just let us have our fun until he felt it was time to stop it. Let's clean up." Since Tom was in his sixth year, I figured that he knew what he was talking about, and I felt a lot better to think that Father Clancy wasn't really steamed at us, and that he knew what was going on from the get-go and gave us some time to have fun.

*

As the school year came to a close, the seminarians from Arkansas who were college-age and older had one last job to do: We were to work a week at St. John's during the retreat that all the diocesan priests in the state were to attend. We knew that a retreat for priests was to be for them a step away from everyday life, with conferences and time for prayer to re-charge the sacerdotal batteries. We who were in our first year as workers were told that we would tidy up the priests' rooms early in the morning while they were attending a Mass said by Bishop Fletcher; we would attend them as they ate breakfast, clean up the refectory after they were finished (and at lunch and supper), and we were to assist them in other ways as requested. If I heard it once, I heard it half-a-dozen times from my brother Arkansas seminarians who had experience at retreats: "Don't be scandalized by anything you see or hear."

Scandalized? That means shocked by something that seems improper—or immoral. How could we be scandalized during the retreat? None of our older seminarians would go any further than to say, "Just don't be scandalized!" I haven't yet figured out how a person who witnesses bad behavior isn't to be offended or shocked by it. Does one just say over and over to himself, "I'm not scandalized!"? I was in the dark about that message from our elders.

The first duty that we carried out for the priests, who were driving in from all over the state on a Sunday afternoon, was to carry their bags from their cars to their assigned rooms. We had a list of the priests' names and the room to which each was assigned. My experience with priests was confined to Little Rock, primarily those who served in my home parish of Holy Souls and those who taught at Catholic High. So there were lots of Arkansas priests I had never seen, though some I had heard of.

There were the brothers whose family name was Maus. The story was that one of them had served mostly urban parishes and the other in rural spots. They were thus referred to as "City Maus and Country Maus." Another priest whose name I had heard in invariably unpleasant contexts was supposed to be "hell on wheels" for any young priest unfortunate enough to be assigned to be his assistant pastor. His reputation included his supposed stalking of his assistant. When an assistant would leave the rectory to drive somewhere, the pastor would tail him, checking to see if he went to the destination were he had informed the pastor (as he was required to do) he was heading. One assistant, according to legend, being followed down the highway, suddenly accelerated at top speed, leaving the older priest behind. Turning into a side street and then making a u-turn, the assistant headed back in the direction of the car and driver that were attempting to catch up, leaning out of his window and waving at the pastor as they drove in opposite directions.

The first priest I can remember assisting was one I didn't know, who grumbled his name when I asked for it as I was unloading two (big!) suitcases from his trunk. I didn't understand him, and I got the impression that he thought I ought to know who he was. He virtually barked it at me when I inquired a second time. He made a comment when I led him to his room that he didn't like it, though being an Arkansas priest he was bound to have stayed in just such a room when he was a seminarian. How it should have been better, I could only guess.

The word among my fellow seminarians was that virtually every priest for whom one toted a suitcase (or two) to his room would hand over a tip of a buck or two. My first priest to assist apparently hadn't heard of the custom. So I headed back to the parking area to help the next new arrival. I was waiting there with a priest who had just arrived to unlock his trunk when I felt a jab in my shoulder from behind. I turned quickly, surprised and wondering what had caused a painful stabbing feeling. There stood Father So-and-So, my first new friend among the Arkansas clergy. Ignoring the fact that another priest was then waiting for me to get his bag, the backstabber said, "There's a damn door under my mattress!"

The beds at St. John's consisted of thin mattresses held up by springs, springs that in some cases sagged noticeably as a result of years and tons of use. To keep from sinking and being enveloped by the mattress, seminarians who had such sorry underpinnings sometimes used wooden slats to add support. This was the first I had heard of a door being used, and I recall thinking it probably provided extremely firm support and struck me as a good idea, though how and where one would acquire a door I didn't know.

I must have been cogitating too long on the impression that the clever solution to sagging made on me, because the not-so-pleasant priest gruffly ordered me to remove the door. I promised to do so as soon as I finished my unloading duties. He then stalked away, and the priest who had been calmly waiting while the complainant lodged his gripe, said, "Don't mind him. He's a grouch." It wasn't quite "Don't be scandalized," but it reminded me of it.

We were to wait upon the guests-for-a-week at assigned tables in the refectory. My second occasion to be scandalized occurred there. It didn't take long at the first meal, Sunday at supper, for me to detect that two priests sitting together at my table were both closing in on a state of drunkenness, within a couple of hours after their arrival. Meals during a retreat are to be conducted in silence by the retreatants, as they were to chew on their food and on the ideas that were emerging from the mouth of one of their brother priests who was reading aloud to all assembled, a custom known as "spiritual reading." Texts were no doubt chosen for the uplifting and insightful observations that they contained about one's relationship with God. That's what retreats were all about: getting closer to the Big Boss.

Larry and Curly, or maybe it was Moe and Shemp, were carrying on a mumbled conversation during the reading that they probably thought no one else could hear, and they were right, if no one else had been within twenty feet of them. I could tell that after they had attracted the attention of every priest within that radius, most of the listeners just turned away, probably not surprised by the two who were being so outwardly obnoxious. Bishop Fletcher and a couple of other priests were sitting at a table in the front of the room, and he heard the inebriated chatter, too; I'm sure of that because he rang a bell, a bell sitting on his table that was like every bell that ever sat on the desk of every grade school teacher I had; it was used when they wanted to get everyone's attention.

I was surprised by the bell, and then more surprised when the Bishop said, in much nicer words the equivalent of "Shut up!" The two gabby fellows were not so far gone as to fail to hear what was said and to understand it. That they ignored the bishop's directive within a couple of minutes did shock, and yes, scandalize me. Sorry, seminary older brothers, I let it happen this very first day.

The meal ended without the bell being rung again, despite the continuing alcohol-induced murmuring, and I suppose the bishop just didn't want to have to acknowledge with a second ringing that his words were being ignored. But the twosome were separated by breakfast the next morning, and the one who remained at the table to which I was assigned didn't seem to be in his cups at any other meal. I suspect somebody had a heart-to-heart with those garrulous guys.

My Catholic High classmate Charlie Lipsmeyer got scandalized early on as well. It might have been on Tuesday morning that we crossed paths shortly after our early-morning duty of seeing that the priests' rooms were in order while they attended Mass. When I saw Charlie in the hall, he looked positively horrified; he had witnessed something awful. I wanted to know what was wrong but he just shook his head and said nothing. I knew I had to get him to talk; I imagined he might have come across the body of a priest, dead in his room.

Finally he told me what he had seen: Among the rooms to which he was assigned was one of a priest who had once been an assistant for many years in Charlie's parish. A very outgoing priest, personable and friendly, he had been a favorite of Charlie's since he was very young. Charlie told me he went into the priest's room, and he was still there, not at meditation and Mass with the other priests. He was sitting on his bed, in his underwear, tilting back the remains of a fifth of bourbon. Charlie backed out of the room so fast he didn't know if he had even been noticed.

Charlie and I talked a bit about the fact that we had both been scandalized by priests who were drinking, and we discussed it as an occupational hazard for priests who were living on their own in parishes that had no brother priests nearby, nor family members either. It was a sad thing to witness, and worse for those suffering from the disease. I'm sure we both vowed to ourselves not to go down that road if and when we were ordained. And let me add that the huge majority of the priests in attendance were sober, courteous, and impressively attuned to the purpose of the retreat.

My first year in the seminary came to an end a few days later, and despite the depressing parts of the retreat, I felt good about the first year and planned to return in the fall.

III • SIXTH PREP

When I think of the sixth prep dorm, just a few feet across the hall from fifth prep, it seems like a long way, just because the second year at St. John's was so different from the first. For instance, the first memory that popped to my mind about that second year was of a classmate, in the sixth prep dorm, who was on fire. The aforementioned Jakes-Memorial-Award winner Gerald Daly was standing just a few feet away from me. I was at my desk, and he was standing, talking to one or two others. He still had on his cassock, and either he or someone nearby was smoking a cigarette.

Suddenly, from about area of his knees, the height where a cigarette dangling from a hand would be, I saw his cassock burst into flame. To his credit Gerald was out of the cassock within seconds, fortunate in that it was a cassock that snapped rather than buttoned. There must have been at least a dozen (I'm trying not to exaggerate, but it seems like more) snaps on every such cassock. On the other hand, the unfortunate thing about thing about his cassock was that it was made of some synthetic material rather than the cotton of the other, button-up, style. I don't think one needs to be a chemist to speculate that whatever material Gerald's cassock was made of, there was at least one petroleum product involved. The episode scared all who were present, and those who had a flammable cassock were quick to say they'd soon be looking for a replacement.

*

Our dormitory had windows that faced the west, which is where the prepside football field lay, and also north, where there was a tennis court. We were alerted one day that there was an unusual tennis match taking place: Father Everett Ballmann and Father James Drane were the singles opponents. The windows were wide and several, and quickly the two players had an audience as we stood at the window and watched. Our observing turned to shouting, which, at first was mostly rooting. The commentary was at least as fast as the game, and encouraging cries of "good shot!" and "too bad!" took a turn to catcalling: "pretty slow getting that that one!" and "my sister serves harder than that!" It was in the midst of the good-natured cracks that for some inexplicable reason, all the shouters but one took a breath. That's when Charlie Lipsmeyer's lone shout rang out: "Drane, you bastard!"

Though Father Drane was our Latin teacher and put us through the paces fast enough that he could have been described as "demanding," he was a very personable, dynamic teacher, and we liked him—Charlie included. Why those words popped into

Charlie's head, I don't think even he knew. It was meant, if I were to guess, as a silly extravagance that his fellow fans would hear amidst all the other hubbub and find funny. No doubt, it wasn't intended for Father Drane's ears.

But there was NO doubt that he heard them. He started to walk towards our building, and we who had been yelling at the windows were swiftly at other tasks: looking at one's shoes, or earnestly studying Latin, when our dorm door flew open, with Father Drane right behind it; he announced, in easy-to-hear words, "Whoever said that, I want him in my room in one minute!"

I remember that Charlie was sitting on a bed, the lower bunk of twins. Like most of us, he was wearing a tee shirt and his black slacks. Without a word, he stood and put on his cassock. Without a word, not even "Pray for me!" he was gone.

I think Father Drane had, that year, moved to prep side, switching places with Father Ballmann, so Charlie had to climb two flights of stairs to get to the floor where Father Drane lived. Like Charlie, we, his classmates, were all but mute as well. We were afraid that the worst might happen: Charlie might be expelled. Whatever happened, it happened fast. Charlie returned so soon that I feared he had heard, "You're out of here, Buddy!" "Buddy" was Father Drane's catch-all nickname for us. Looking a bit shell-shocked, Charlie told us that he had apologized profusely and, despite some work-detail punishment that was assigned, Father Drane accepted his apology and that was that. Whew!

*

We had a small concession stand in the basement of our building, and from it candy bars and cold drinks were sold. Theft of Snickers and Hershey bars had been discovered, and a plan was made to catch the thief. Chief engineer of the plan was Al Schneider, who had in mind a trap to catch the yegg. When I say Al was *engineer* and was creating a *trap*, I mean the words literally. He went off to a building we called the "powerhouse," a place that featured the boilers that created the steam heat in the winter and also had within it some woodworking tools. When he returned, Al had in hand his handmade rat trap—a marvel of simplicity and design. It was about the size of a shoe box, with a sliding door that could be raised and balanced open by a stick that connected to a second stick that protruded down through a hole in the roof. At the pointed end of that stick, Al attached a bit of Hershey's best. When (and if) that morsel was nibbled, a chain reaction would be set sticks in motion and down would come the door behind the varmint. Would it work? It was mighty impressive in the demonstration Al provided. We would check in the morning, as the new home, we hoped, for the larcenous rodent was put in place alongside some other sweets, but none so readily available, unwrapped, and easy-to-see.

Whether Al checked the trap before or after morning prayers, Mass, and breakfast, I don't know. But it was early in the morning when the word went out: "The trap door is down!" I'm guessing that it was a Saturday, given what followed. Al was holding the closed box and stated that from the weight of it, he was sure "something" was inside. That he wouldn't speculate on what he couldn't see inside gave an air of mystery to the situation, as far as I was concerned, though what else it could have been besides a rat I couldn't imagine.

Wouldn't you know it? Somebody found a perfect receptacle in which we could deposit the captured critter—a birdcage. Actually, *birdscage* would be a better description, as it was capacious and could provide room for two or three robins or blue jays. The door to the cage was opened wide and Al put the trap flush against it. He then pulled up the sliding door—and nothing came out! Somebody tapped on the end of the trap and zoom! out came *Rattus norvegicus* (we were still big into Latin in 1962). It was a good sized brown rat, and as it was now trapped in our sixth prep dorm, it was the center of attention by all residents. I shuddered to think that it might escape into the dorm and hide somewhere, like under my bed.

"So, what next?" The question was apt, and the beast's demise was agreed upon without the necessity of a vote. Whether what followed was the first suggested means to its end or not, I don't know, but the method of extermination that won approval was to suffocate it by encasing the cage in the yards of clear plastic we had on hand from the just-returned-from-the-laundry cassocks that hung here and there in the dorm. I don't know if we liked the idea because it involved no violence or blood, or if we wanted to see it die right before our eyes, twitching and squirming for the last molecules of oxygen. The plastic was gathered, and the cage was soon enveloped in it, and the captive was closely watched as the minutes ticked away. Then more minutes ticked away. After a half hour or more he was as peppy as ever.

"Sulfuric acid!" We could all see the brilliance of the second deadly suggestion. There was a chemistry lab on the premises (for the high schoolers). A few drops of what would be a deadly chemical into that air-tight environment was a fiendish (and cool) idea! I believe that after the administration of the chemical a funky haze developed inside the cage; I am absolutely sure that the surgically inserted drops of the poisonous stuff had no discernable effect on the prisoner. It was as peppy and alive as it had been before what we thought would be the fatal solution was administered. What to do next?

"Drown him!" That was a stroke of genius. We had a creek behind the prep side. It was often two or three feet deep. Even though we knew rats could swim, we would just plunk the cage into and under the slow moving water and let nature take its course. Which it did. A cage that is twenty-four inches at its narrowest, when inserted into twenty inches of water naturally leaves enough room for a rat to swim to the side of the cage and then hold himself there, or to cling, upside down on the top of the cage, out of the H^2O below. Yeah, we got sticks and rapped his little paws, and he'd let go, doing the Australian crawl for a bit, then he'd grab the top again. We were getting nowhere.

"What are you guys doing? This was the inquiry from one of our classmates, call him C.B., one who had apparently missed the morning's excitement, from capture to attempted capital punishment. We explained our futile attempts to lessen the world's rat population by one. "Wait a minute," he ordered. It sounded sort of disdainful. He returned, gunny sack in hand. "Open the door," he said of the cage, holding the gunny sack open as a means of escape for the rat. We fished the jail cell from the creek and did as ordered. The rat saw the opportunity to make a break for it and zipped right into C.B.'s sack, which he quickly twirled in his hand, tightening it at the top. What next?

He took two steps in the direction of the nearest pine tree and, against it, pounded the bag and its contents two or three times. He dropped the bag to the ground and walked off. Well, yeah, I guess you could do it that way.

*

We took English as well as Latin. We had a history of English literature text that discussed great works, when they were written, and by whom, and what trends they did or didn't follow. The only thing missing was the works themselves. Honestly, the text was suitable for a history class I suppose (dry as the Sahara, though it was), but it failed miserably to present any literature itself. It was therefore a welcome relief when our teacher announced that we were each to write a short story, and some of them would be read in class. At last, relief from the textbook!

So we all buckled down, grabbed paper and pen, and in a couple of weeks all had a story to read. Mike O'Malley had recently read J. D. Salinger's *The Catcher in the Rye*, so his protagonist referred to things as *crappy* and *miserable*, and more than a few *damns* punctuated the tale as well. We thought Mike was pretty daring to emulate Holden Caulfield's lingo.

Since not all the stories would be read in class, several of us read our creations aloud in the dorm. Among the readers was C.B., the rat killer himself, and he read us a story that astounded me when I heard it. It was about a man and woman who had become pen pals and had apparently fallen in love, courtesy of Uncle Sam's postal service. They were soul mates, so they made an appointment to meet. She would arrive by bus in his home town. He would meet her at the station. They agreed that they would each wear a red rose, hers pinned to her jacket, his inserted in the buttonhole of his coat's lapel, to identify themselves. Before she arrived, the man decided to test her claim to love him by paying a guy, a plain looking, heavy-set fellow who worked at the station, to wear the rose. He told the employee it was a trick he was playing on a traveler who would arrive soon. He gave him his coat to wear. The pen-pal lover wanted to see if she would approach him even if he wasn't especially good-looking.

Off the bus she got, a woman who was herself rather ordinary looking, not that it mattered to him, so in love with her had he fallen. When she spotted the man hired to wear the rose, she went to him immediately. As they stood before each other, the lover stepped up to the woman as she was facing the hired rose-wearer, and said, "I'm Bill, the guy you've been writing." At that, a pretty woman standing nearby took the place of the woman wearing the rose and said, "And I'm Betty, the woman you've been writing."

Man! That story was so good that everybody who was listening looked at each other in astonishment. Who knew that C.B. had such a story to tell? Well, one of our classmates did. "Good story, C.B., and I liked it when I read it in *Saturday Evening Post*, too."

*

One of the new guys in sixth prep was Roland Lajoie, from Maine. I remember Roland for his good humor and slight accent, a bit of French in it. One day, surely a Saturday again, he proposed to show us something amazing. Somehow he had come into possession of two pocketknives. He wanted to know if anyone would volunteer to take them, seat himself on the floor, and then Roland would astonish all observers. I volunteered.

I sat on the wooden floor (well, well worn!) of our dorm, my legs spread far apart, as instructed. Roland had a small cup of water from which he poured a few ounces, between my legs, within a couple of inches of where my legs began to separate into a V. A small rag in hand, he directed that I should open the knife blades, and jab them up and down in the area just beyond my knees to prevent his hands from getting to the water, which he said he could wipe up.

"You're crazy," I told him. My reflexes were still good enough at the advanced age of nineteen to prevent him from getting to the water. And so we began, with Roland on his knees, me on my derriere, quickly striking the blades to the floor, separating him from the water. "You're never going to be able to do this. Stop, before I accidentally stab you!" I declared, as he made a few futile, feinting attempts to get past the fast-moving knives. That's when he grabbed me by the ankles and pulled me, shocked, towards him, the backside of my Levi's doing exactly what he said he would do: dry up the water. Got me last!

P.S. Roland was ordained for the Marist order and as of 2015 was a pastor in Tampa, Florida.

*

One of my standard ways of telling a story about someone to preserve his anonymity was to say, "I can't reveal his name because it would embarrass his mother, Mrs. Lipsmeyer." So, adhering to that policy, I relate that one of my sixth prep fellows, name not to be mentioned, decided to take a dare. For one thing, there was money to be had. He estimated for me, checking with him on the details fifty-four years after the event, that it might have been "two dollars and seventy-six cents." For that amount of money he was to run from prep side to the football field, a distance of probably fifty yards—and back. Did I mention that he was to be naked?

And so this young man, in full light of day (a fact that I will provide later will convince you that it *was* daytime) took off for the objective, wearing as we used to say, "only his birthday suit," and made it back, happy, I'm sure that he was almost three dollars to the good. But then, less happy, when one of the high school lads informed him that he had taken his picture as he sped back to the sem. Since it is unlikely that the photographer had an infra-red camera, or whatever those devices are called that can take pictures in the dark, I can assure you it took place, as they also say, "in broad daylight."

When the creator of the pix asked for payment to hand over the developed copy of the shot, the anonymous streaker was threatened with the loss of the bounty he had earned by his sprint. As a matter of fact, the lad who ran the naked reverse actually was shown the picture about a week later by the would-be black-mailer, which Mr. Natural ruefully acknowledged was a reasonable likeness of him—all of him. The extortionist was apparently kidding about extracting any cash and handed over the photo to him who was the subject, presumably a portrait soon shredded. The negative, however, may still be in existence.

*

St. John's had two football fields. So there were plenty of wide open spaces. At Heights Variety Store up on Kavanaugh, I bought a box kite and a ball of string one windy Saturday afternoon. I don't think I had ever flown a box kite before that day, so I wasn't sure of its particulars as far as getting it to fly was concerned. Did I need to attach a cloth tail? I was told it wasn't necessary. I and another fan of flight quickly assembled the kite and tied the ball of string to the proper place on the kite as identified by printed directions. We were on the upper side football field (interloping prep siders!) and a strong southerly wind was ablowin'. It was late afternoon, maybe twenty minutes before supper time.

The kite took off amazingly well, and we let out more and more of our string supply until I would have sworn that the high flier had gone far enough north that it must have been over the Arkansas River! The river, however might have been a mile away, and our string supply was something less than that. But it was high, I tell you, not exactly a spot in the sky, but profoundly diminished in size as it danced. Eventually we heard the bell for supper. The kite was tugging hard on our connection. We would probably be late if we tried to bring it in. Just let it go? We hated the thought of that, so we took a few steps in the direction of a fence-enclosed basketball court and tied the string to the fence, knowing that when it fell during supper we had only a tiny chance of recovering it.

When we finished eating, we went to try to recover our kite. That it was still flying was an unexpected and happy surprise!

*

October 22, 1962 was the night President Kennedy spoke on television and radio about the presence of Russian missiles in Cuba. The news was met at St. John's, as everywhere else in the country, with much concern. In the days following, as tensions rose, I heard a couple of guys saying that if we went to war with the Russians, they would quit the seminary and sign up for the military. Though I wasn't especially well informed about nuclear weapons, I had seen pictures of Hiroshima and Nagasaki after the atom bombs fell. So I was pretty sure that if an all-out nuclear conflict broke out, there wouldn't be much need for more men in the military as much as there would be, for any who survived such a battle, willing people to try to help deal with the devastation that would follow. Happily, the situation eventually was defused, but it had a lasting impact on me in terms of how different and dangerous those weapons were and continue to be. It had been pointed out to me that, for the first time in the history of warfare, a weapon fired with intent to harm didn't have to hit the intended targets directly. Its radioactive fallout could kill days after it was first exploded. The world was fortunate that disaster was averted.

*

Father Drane, as I mentioned, was our Latin teacher, and as I also noted, his classes were very lively and interesting. He was a dynamic, young, slim import from the Philadelphia area, a place so flush with the number of vocations to the priesthood that they could share some of their bounty with the diocese of Little Rock. He was teaching both fifth and sixth prep guys in the same class. I especially recall that he was grimly determined, despite obvious roadblocks (i.e., our blockheads), that we would master a Latin doozy called "ablative absolute." It was a common expression among the old Romans, it seemed, but one which our English-speaking minds couldn't readily grasp. To this day Mike O'Malley shakes his head as if trying to make an unpleasant idea go away whenever I mention the construction, which I do from time to time just to watch him flinch.

I also mentioned that Father Drane commonly called many of us "Buddy." I bring it up again to connect it with an incident in Latin class. A fifth prep fellow with a very Irish name like O'Shea was called "Mr. Green" instead of "Buddy" by Father Drane. It was invariable: "Mr. Green, can you decline *imperator*?" "Mr. Green, what is the object of the preposition in that sentence?" One day after being so-called, O'Shea had had it. "Father Drane, why do you insist on calling me 'Mr. Green'? My name is O'Shea!" It was obvious the boy was upset. One could hear from his tone that his feelings were hurt.

Father Drane could hear it, too. He paused, seeming to hunt for the words that followed. "Mr. O'Shea, I call you 'Mr. Green' because I have a terrible memory for names. You may have noticed that I call a lot of you guys 'Buddy.' That's because I can't remember what your real names are. You, at least, I can remember that your name is Irish, and when I think of Ireland I think of green. So you're 'Mr. Green.' That's more than I can remember about lots of guys. So I'm not trying to insult you by calling you 'Mr. Green.' It's just the best I can do—at least up to now. I really wish my memory was better. I'm sorry."

O'Shea and the rest of us were startled by the confession. During the next class Father Drane asked, "Mr. O'Shea, can you define *impedimentum*?"

*

Speaking of the classical lingo, and reminding you of the earlier linkage of the names Drane and Lipsmeyer, Charlie was, of course, in the class that was eagerly taking in as much of Latin as possible. When it was obvious that time enough had passed that the Drane-Lipsmeyer tennis court oath had been forgotten by the principals involved, that bygones had indeed become bygones, Charlie was taking an afternoon nap (in the dorm, of course) when he startled those of us present by mumbling in his sleep. We were amused by his mumbled locutions, but as they continued, they became clearer. From the sleeping lad's lips we distinctly heard, "*Esse aut non esse, illa est questio.*" Good grief! Charlie was quoting the famous line that Hamlet spoke when he was debating whether to kill himself or not. Ben Jonson, an English writer, wrote that the illustrious Shakespeare knew "little Latin," and yet here was Charlie reciting the Bard's words in that very tongue. That's when somebody's crap detector kicked in: "Lipsmeyer, you phony, don't try to make us think you're dreaming in Latin!" Smiling broadly, Charlie sat up, and we all had a good laugh.

*

pre-1961: From seminary lore comes the following tale: The library was once located on the ground floor in the front of Morris Hall (the main building, named for the bishop who built the seminary). Two doors had access to the library, one of which was from inside the building, the other from the outside. Both doors were locked each night. Despite that, someone got into the library two nights in a row, knocking books to the floor. How the prankster or pranksters got in was a mystery, except for the fact that there were four or five windows in the room, one of which must have been left unlocked, despite the order (from Monsignor Aretz, the rector) after the first incident to make sure those windows were secure.

When something was amiss at St. John's, when things departed from the usual expectations of where they should be located or how they should appear, the culprits who were suspected of disrupting the smooth running of life were invariably identified as "neighborhood kids." The rector called all the seminarians together after the second intrusion to let them know that the usual suspects were, indeed, "neighborhood kids," but he warned them that if any seminarians were involved in tossing the books about, they had better desist, because he himself was going to guard the library that night.

The next morning, the rector didn't show up to say the morning Mass. Knowing smiles were exchanged among the seminarians waiting for him in the chapel. He no doubt had fallen asleep on the job in the library. The senior man of the seminary was sent, key to the library in hand, to wake up the snoozing watchman. When the senior man entered the library he saw two things: books on the floor and the wide-eyed rector staring at them. Sorry to say, the unsatisfying denouement is that Monsignor Aretz never spoke of what he saw nor were the books ever disturbed again.

*

One of my Catholic High basketball teammates—who was a year younger than I—started at St. John's in my second year. Harrigan Wortsmith was the brother of Cathy, whom I had taken to the prom when we were seniors. Cathy was, in 1962, in her second year at the St. Louis convent run by the Religious Sisters of Mercy, on her way to becoming a nun.

In his junior year at C.H.S., Harrigan had suffered a severely broken leg in a freak accident when he and an opposing player ran into each other in the semi-finals of the state basketball tournament. So bad was the injury that he wasn't able to play football at all during his senior year. That was a shame because he was an outstanding halfback with extraordinary speed and equally good ability to catch a pass.

By the time he got to St. John's, however, Harrigan seemed to have regained his former fleetness, and when the Home-Foreign Game came around, it was time to exploit it. I was, for lack of a really good passer, still the quarterback of the Home prep siders. During the game, over and over I had "H," as I called him, run straight at the unfortunate defensive back assigned to try to guard him, and then he'd cut sharply to the sideline, where I'd mange to get him the ball. On at least two occasions we added a wrinkle. I'd fake that pass to my future brother-in-law (I add what is probably obvious: that Cathy, my prom date, left the convent after thirteen years as a nun, as I did the seminary after four, and we eventually got married).

Back to football. The pass route involving the fake throw is known as "down, out, and down," and as soon as I'd pretend I was going to throw that sideline pass, Harrigan would cut upfield and I'd chunk the ball as far as I could, knowing that he was fast enough to catch up with it. The resulting touchdowns were an important part of the second win in a row for the Home team!

*

Have you ever known anyone who walked on the Arkansas River? The rumor at the sem in the winter of 1962 was that the river had frozen out a few feet. Being from Missouri, I had to be shown that it was so. The weekend was upon us, and though the frigid temps had been harsh on those who ventured out, the prospect of a walk down the hill to the river promised to warm our bones and to provide an answer to the question, "Is the river really frozen?" So we went, the four of us. I remember only one other lad's name, and I'll mention it shortly.

Despite the exercise needed to get to the "old man," it was still pretty dadgum chilly when we arrived at the riverside. I guesstimate that it might be a mile from St. John's to that point—all downhill, so the effort to get there wasn't rigorous. We were still extremely cold. Nevertheless, on with an experiment, which would be to try to walk on the surface. Since I was the instigator of the excursion, it was my duty to test to see if the rumor was true. The river's edge did look to be unmoving, as did the river a few feet out. If it wasn't moving, that had to be because it was frozen—right?

So, out I stepped, not putting more than 150 pounds worth of total weight on the surface, though I have no idea how to figure the translation of my body weight to pounds per square inch at the soles of my basketball shoes. First one foot, then the other. It held! It was true, the river was frozen. I didn't venture out more than a couple of feet, but all present were in agreement: The Arkansas River was frozen; in my mind since I took two steps upon it, that constituted walking. So if you hadn't known anybody before this moment who walked on the Arkansas River, now you do. My chum on the adventure whose name I here insert was David Mikeska, a tall, lean fellow from Longview, Texas. He decided to make history as well ("The First Texan to…").

Dave was wearing boots, but they weren't cowboy boots. They were shorter and plainer than what would fit the stereotype of a Texan's footwear, but they sure seemed much more appropriate to the day's activity than my Chuck Taylors. Dave also went on to the ice gingerly. Did I mention that Dave probably weighed twenty-five pounds more than I did? That likely had to do with the fact that in less than five seconds of his taking two steps (and thus, by my definition, *walking*) onto the ice, smiling at the three of us as he did, the ice gave way, and he was immediately halfway up to his knees in freezing water.

His open-topped boots provided a clear channel into which the freezing water could pour, and we dragged him on his tail end out of the river and on to the shore. I knew from the look on his face that the icy overflow inside his boots was excruciating, and we yanked off his footwear as fast as we could to empty out the unwelcome water. No sooner did we get the boots off than we shoved them right back on his feet, as we all agreed that we needed to get back to St. John's pronto. We didn't want what started off as a lark to turn into something really unfortunate.

By the time we huffed and puffed our way uphill to the top of it, where the seminary lay, the effort needed brought about the warmth (and then some!) that we had expected the downhill trek would have provided. Dave was stalwart going back, answering patiently and affirmatively our repeated inquiries, "Are you OK?" He took a hot shower and suffered no lasting ill effects. Even though more than five decades have passed since that day, I bet that David Mikeska is still "The *Only* Texan Who...."

*

At mid-term of our sixth prep year we got a new class-mate: Ron Harry Beale (not exactly his name). A bit on the rotund side, he was rosy-cheeked and very genial. Said his last stop had been Regis College in Denver. Unpacked an impressive array of books—among them, a large number dealing with canon (church) law. His "hobby," he said. Wow! Only the guys in the major seminary studied canon law! We welcomed him, and soon he became just another sixth prepper, though he differed from us in that he seemed to need very little time for study compared to the rest of us. We figured he was some kind of prodigy. Who else would have canon law as a hobby? He told us he had Jewish relatives or that he was part Jewish, and it wasn't long before he was in contact with some very influential Jews in Little Rock, including the local rabbi.

He also made contact with some Jewish store owners who had businesses near the seminary. One, a woman who owned what now would be thought of as a boutique food business, sup-plied him with some exotic samples (or so we assumed) from her store. Given the state of our food supply at "He Knows Faith," more than a few of us envied Ron Harry (who invariably used both given names when identifying or speaking of himself).

It wasn't long before Ron Harry was hard at work on an event: He wanted us seminarians to put on a Seder, which is a Jew-ish ceremony that begins Passover, the celebration of the Jews' escape from Egyptian slavery. In an era when many denomina-tions of Christians, as well as Christians and Jews, were looking for common ground and promoting unity in a movement iden-tified as *ecumenical*, such a performance by St. John's students would be much in keeping with the spirit of the times.

I have no idea what steps Ron Harry took to get the Seder underway, from acquiring approval of our rector, to the use our small gymnasium for the event, to the enlistment of faculty members, Father Drane among them, to promote it in Little Rock. What I do know is that before long several of us from sixth prep had been recruited by Ron Harry to participate in the Seder, Ron Harry procured (from who-knows-where) copies of *Haggadah*, the book that contained the Seder rituals and prayers. Soon we were learning the lines that made up the ritual, with Ron Harry playing the lead role of the father of a family, which included his singing in Hebrew. We portrayed the children.

We practiced a number of times until we had it down. Came the night in April, as I recall, when the event was to take place, and the sight was amazing! The ancient gym, cleaned as best as it could be, was filled with folding chairs that may have numbered 200. At one end was a raised platform on which we participants would sit and perform. We all wore our regulation seminarian black suit, white shirt, and black tie. We heard a rumor that turned out to be true: that a national Catholic magazine had both a reporter and photographer on the scene. In a later month we saw the proof in black and white.

How Ron Harry managed it all is beyond my imagining. Our rector was there, sitting in the front row next to the rabbi. Well dressed adults from both the Jewish and Christian communities filed in. The gym began to fill, and what seats weren't taken by guests were occupied by deacons and other older seminarians. The Seder went as planned; the guests were generous in their applause at the ceremony's end. Our performance, and that, of course, is what it was, since we were not Jews, was written up the next day in the local papers, accompanied by a picture of Ron Harry.

The aftermath of the extraordinary night was less successful. We saw that Ron Harry received shockingly bad results from tests administered in our various classes. Then he got more of them. Then he was gone—left—departed, all before the second semester had ended. Then we began to hear stories about unpaid bills—things he had charged to the seminary without anyone's awareness, much less approval. One of the bills, apparently, from the woman who owned the food store, where R.H.B. had a charge account. Ron Harry disappeared from our lives as he had entered them: unexpectedly.

When I heard a few years ago of Leonardo DiCaprio's film "Catch Me If You Can," about a chameleon-like character who shifts from one identity to another, it put me in mind of Ron Harry Beale, and I wondered where he ended up—or if he had ended up anywhere, yet.

*

You might have heard athletes speaking about "being in the zone." My understanding of what they mean when they use the term is playing at a level of positive results that go beyond anything that is ordinary. So, regardless of the sport, when a guy is in the zone, he's "hot." Joe DiMaggio in 1941 got base hits in 56 straight games—obviously, he was "in the zone." I found myself there once, and it was at St. John's.

Despite the fact that very few people at St. John's, outside of the participants, cared a whit about the results of any intramural basketball game, it did matter to those of us who competed. Giving it the "old seminary try" was expected among the players. We tried our best, and winning was the goal. I'm telling you this because I want my one and only time in that mysterious region not to be construed as coming in a game where nobody was really making an effort. That would make my bragging even less impressive.

The only specifics I can remember from that day—the day the zone made its unique visit to me in all the games of basketball, football, and baseball that I played as a boy, and the golf and racquetball that I still play—is that my team won, and that I made every shot I took. There is one more memory that I believe is accurate, and it's that a fellow who later was related to me by marriage was guarding me from time to time.

*

pre-1961: When a priest in the diocese of Little Rock (which included the entire state) died, it was the custom to bring his body to St. John's where he would lie in state for a day until his funeral arrangements could be carried out. The story I was told is that a priest died (what I would assume was a peaceful death) sitting in a chair. Not found for a day or two until after his last day, the man had extreme rigor mortis. So extreme was the corpse's seated position, and so determinedly did it resist the laying out that is necessary for a body to fit into a coffin, that the undertakers (this happened before "funeral directors" came into existence) had to use piano wire to hold Father So-and-So in the required supine position.

The body of a dead priest in the chapel was not ever to be alone, so a list was posted for four seminarians per hour to prayerfully attend the deceased. Seminarians, starting on the upper side, signed up to take specific hours. The foursome keeping vigil would position themselves on kneelers that were placed two per side of the casket, which was resting on a bier. As you might imagine, when the list was eventually brought to prep side for the younger seminarians to volunteer, all the reasonable time periods were already taken. So the earliest morning hours were all that was left for the youngest to fill.

It was at such an hour, say 3:00 a.m., that the four high school boys, kneeling in prayer next to the dead priest, heard the twang of the piano wire as it broke and saw the body sit upright in the casket.

*

The 1962 version of the above is the same in a couple of particulars: The dead priest was in the main chapel, and the attendees at the coffin in the pre-dawn hours were high schoolers. The variance to the previous tale (none of which I can vouch for as having happened) is that sometime after midnight a couple of upper side jokers sneaked into the choir loft which was just above the casket one floor below and proceeded to empty out the chapel of the four living souls below by means of low, pained moans.

*

I have mentioned that, to me, the food wasn't dependably good beyond the boxes of cereal and the toast at breakfast. I acknowledge being then (and now) a picky eater, but there was a night when my gustatory judgment was borne out by others.

In my opinion, naming the chow hall after the Little Rock bishop named Byrne is getting the place off to a bad start. Then, as I previously reported, to try to run the operation on less than two dollars a day per person also adds to the likelihood that the cuisine isn't going to be good. The events that follow cemented in my mind that whoever created the "He Knows Faith" alternative name hit the nail on the head. The night that I have in mind to represent the straw that broke the camel's back (or the entrée that prompted a visit to the rector about the menu) began as any other night, with the fellows who were assigned as waiters for that week delivering bowls of food to the tables. So out came the green beans, and out came the potatoes. Last, and least, out came the liver.

Could I eat a piece of liver with death as the alternative? I suppose so. But nobody had a gun on me that night, and I passed on it as soon as I heard what it was. I didn't even look at it. But somebody at my table did. "It's swimming in grease!" was his observation. Whether that was so or not, I don't know, but his and my unwillingness to sample it was then supported by a third and fourth vote. Then it was unanimous. Our waiter was told, "Take it back. " He didn't ask why, which indicates to me that he may have known as soon as he picked up the bowl that its contents weren't going to be popular. He headed for the kitchen, the bowl in his hands. Then we saw other waiters doing the same. Then it was all the waiters from the prep side dining room returning the liver. One came back quickly and said, "The upper siders are doing the same. And the senior man over there came into the kitchen while I was there and explained to the head cook that it wasn't her fault that the liver was coming back. She just didn't have enough of a budget."   •

The next day a delegation went to the rector and complained about the food. I have, unfortunately, no memory of it ever getting better, but I also don't recall a meal as bad as that which we saw on "Take Back the Liver Night."

*

We were shocked to hear that two of the longest attending seminarians for the diocese of Little Rock who were in first philosophy had decided, within days of each other, to leave before the second semester was over. It was the seventh year at St. John's for both of them. Monsignor O'Connell, the rector, must have been dismayed that the young men who had been at St. John's since they were ninth graders were leaving. My conclusion that the rector was upset at the news has to do with the day after both were gone.

Cecil Moix, a classmate of the two who had just departed, was from Conway and thus he was a candidate for the Arkansas priesthood; he went to the rector's office and requested time to speak to him. My imagined conversation, one that the rector must have feared was about the departure of the third Arkansas seminarian, is based on what Cecil reported in the aftermath:

Msgr. O'C: "Cecil, what's on your mind?"

Cecil: "Monsignor, I was wondering if the seminary would pay for one or two bales of straw so we could put targets on them for bow and arrow shooting? It should cost about eight to ten dollars."

Msgr. O'C: "Cecil, you can buy four or five of them!"

*

It was in sixth prep that I began to understand the excellence of the teachers at St. John's. Many were home-grown, and not only were they classroom stars, they were admirable men, models for those of us aspiring to the priesthood. In no particular order I mention, first, Father Clancy, our prepside boss who taught Sociology and Catholic Social Justice courses. Father Clancy was not only one to teach about society, but he was also one engaged with it. He was a known local voice for racial justice—and not alone among St. John's teachers for that involvement. Fathers Drane and Ballmann, were masters of their subject matter (Latin and Philosophy for the former, Old and New Testaments the latter). Father David Boileau was the heavyweight in the Philosophy department; his Ph.D. in the subject was from the prestigious Catholic University of Louvain in Belgium. He was a mountain of a man, maybe 6'8", possessed of a booming voice and a confidence that may have derived from his intellect and physique. Three of the men mentioned in this paragraph eventually left the priesthood, Father Boileau being the exception. He taught for years at Loyola in New Orleans.

Fathers James Nugent and Joseph Biltz were admired by the major seminarians for their theological expertise and even more for their character. "What a man!" I heard more than one theologian say of Father Nugent. Father Biltz, though soft-spoken, was the Catholic voice heard loudest in Little Rock on civil rights. He told me that he once sat across the table from a local business leader who was anything but enthusiastic about racial equality. At some point in their heated discussion of the issue the man pulled out a pistol and put it on the table. "I was pretty sure he was going to use it," Father Biltz said in as calm a way as I could imagine.

We prep siders enjoyed the English classes we took the first two years of college primarily because of the markedly different but interesting men who taught us: Father Joseph Walsh and Father Patrick Lynch. Father Walsh was a dynamic fellow, willing to listen to and debate questions we raised. The rule at St. John's was that one had to wait in the classroom for ten minutes if the professor was late. At a second after that, we could exit the room—class cancelled! Father Walsh informed us that in our prep side classroom we had to look out our windows and watch for him to exit his upper side living quarters. If he was visible before the ten-minute limit, we had to stay. We were convinced that he had a stop watch in his pocket that he set for just shy of ten minutes, as time and again we groaned as he popped out the door with only seconds to spare. Father Lynch, on the other hand, was a mellow, laid-back fellow, who was often amazed and sometimes appalled by our ignorance. It was his habit to light up a Lucky Strike or two during the class, making the smokers among us itchy for one themselves, so thoroughly did he seem to enjoy it. One day, as he heard one wrong response after another to a question that he was *sure* we ought to be able to answer, he rose from his desk, walked to the open window, leaned on the sill, took a drag from his cigarette, pondered silently for what was surely more than a minute, and finally said to us, "Some days, all you can do is smoke."

*

"*Tu es bonus sed totus*," was the invention of one of my classmates. It makes little sense literally translated: "You are good but whole." If ever a faint compliment and an open insult were married, this is it. The sentence began life as an amusing, gentle jab, but eventually it was abbreviated to *sed totus* and used about someone (chiefly, C.B., the rodent exterminator) as strictly a revilement. But after he left the seminary, there was another evolution: It became a friendly put-down, which is where it has remained among those of us who see each other and occasionally address each other with it—Al, Mike, and me. Weird, eh?

*

One of the guys in first philosophy had become known to us the year before when he was in sixth prep as a volatile fellow. He was capable of and sometimes given to powerful outbursts of feeling—of many kinds. He could be noticeably angry, happy, upset, or frustrated. Because of that, when he, I, and two others had a chance to play golf (the circumstances of which completely elude me, just in case you're wondering when, in a seminarian's schedule, such would be possible), I suggested to the other two guys that we put to use an exploding golf ball. Remember, by this time we had thoroughly soaked up the idea that a good prank at St. John's was an achievement worth celebrating, telling, and re-telling.

I was credited with a dandy idea! How I came to have such a ball at home, I don't know, and the details of how I got it from there are foggy, but the fact was that when our foursome began a round at Rebsamen Golf Course, I had it in my bag. Mr. Emotion, call him Fred for short, was going to blow his top if we could get him to hit the ball made entirely of chalk. The trio of plotters picked a golfy sort of term, like *double-eagle*, and when that was said, it was the cue for the plot to unfold. My two comrades were to distract Fred just after he teed up his ball, intending to whack it far down the fairway with his driver. They had to get him to turn away from his ball and to walk a step or two away from it. That's when I would swoop down and replace the Titleist with the Chalkie.

I think the ruse involved calling Fred over to see if he could identify a snake, which would be conveniently gone when he got to the spot. It worked perfectly. I swapped the balls, and we all stood back and waited for Fred to hit. It was going to be a riot— as, first, the ball and then Fred would explode!

Back from not seeing the imaginary snake, Fred, his knees bent, driver placed behind the bomb, I mean the *ball*, eyed his target. Then he moved his head slightly toward it, a quizzical look on his face. Then it was all over. He bent down, took the ball (which, being chalk, weighed less than half what a regulation ball did and was much whiter than his) and said, "What's going on?" Quietly, calmly, soberly. Vesuvius was not going to erupt that day. "The best laid plans…"

*

The school year '62-'63 was history except for a little thing called "final exams." When someone suggested a stint of extra-legal, post-lights-out study for the final "final," I agreed to be part of the clandestine group of procrastinators. Finding a spot to carry out this nefarious proposal was problematic. The building offered very few out-of-the-way places that were lighted. One of the group of four that had formed for this purpose made a strange suggestion, at least it seemed strange to me: the prep side football field.

I can't recall the process by which the threesome answered my several questions: Where? How lighted? What if we're seen from the main building? What I do remember is that after lights out, the four of us took turns exiting our dorm for ostensible visits to the jakes, hoping that no one noticed that we didn't return—or cared if he did notice. I assume we had our books stashed somewhere to gather up as we hiked to the field. In an area of the field previously scouted out by at least one of the group but not yet seen by me, we huddled behind a short wall of some sort that prevented us from being seen by drivers or walkers along Taylor Street, which was the western boundary of St. John's property. Handily, the space was also behind hedges or shrubs that virtually blocked the view of it from Fitzgerald Hall, prep side's official name.

And we did have light, a lantern of some kind I suppose. We were all cramming for the last test in a class called History of Education, a course that wasn't nearly as interesting as its title suggests. What amazes me now is that I think we were up most of the night, firing questions at each other, and chanting lists together, e.g., "the seven main educational advances of the 18th century were…," keeping each other awake, and generally lamenting that we had to take a test in such a dreary subject.

We skulked back to the dorm before daylight, entering as we left, individually. Thinking we had managed to make our departure and return unnoticed, I rolled into my bottom bunk, wishing that I had more than a few minutes to lie there before the first bell of the day rang. That's when I heard a whispered, "Welcome back." We weren't as undetected as we thought.

The exam was in the morning, probably two hours long. My two sharpest memories of the experience were that my first all-night-awake experience left me totally exhausted, and that the chigger bites I had unknowingly acquired on the field were beginning to make themselves known. The infernal itching that I experienced the last thirty minutes or so of the test is what I credit for keeping me from placing my head on the desk, unanswered questions be damned.

The lesson I learned about all-night "study" was sufficient to keep me from a repeat performance until years later in graduate school. And the second time turned out no better than the first, as my thinking was both fuzzy and obsessively fixed upon taking a nap.

Thus ended my sixth prep year at St. John's, but my respite from academe was short-lived. Father Boileau, the bellwether of the Philosophy department, had summer-school plans for several Arkansans, including me.

*

Father Boileau spearheaded a movement to make sure that priests from the Little Rock diocese who might end up teaching had degrees in secular subjects from accredited college programs. That's why five of us took off for Fayetteville and the University of Arkansas and its summer school. Al Schneider and I were the two from prep side, and Larry Frederick, Scherry Cardwell, and Dick Strock were from the upper side. The subjects we studied varied from history to math to Spanish to English. Of the three older fellows, I knew that Larry had gone to Catholic High a few years before me. Scherry and Dick I knew only by sight.

The quintet lived at the Newman Center, the Catholic outreach to students at UA. The pastor there was Father John

O'Dwyer, who made us feel welcome. The cook and house-keeper at the center was Mrs. Pond, and the fact that her work had increased five-fold never seemed to bother her. She was always nice to us, though we were clearly a group the like of which she had never experienced before—we were known to her as "seminars."

One of my first Fayetteville encounters with Larry Frederick (now a monsignor, the rector of and fabled teacher at Catholic High and Mt. St. Mary's) proved to be instructive. I learned that he was a fellow who took his duty seriously, a trait he has practiced throughout his adult life.

I must have forgotten to bring an alarm clock. That would explain why I asked him to wake me in the morning for our first day of class. He did that, of course, exactly, I'm sure, at whatever time I requested. I felt him shake me slightly that first day and announce the time. I rolled over, saw him through squinting eyes, and thanked him. I noticed, in a few seconds, my eyes opening again, that he was still standing by my bedside. "Why are you still here?" I mumbled. "I'm not leaving until your feet hit the floor," he explained. As I said, "seriously."

The summer of '63 remains a happy memory for me because of the young men with whom I spent it. I already knew, liked, and admired Al, our two years together on prep side having cemented in my mind that he was a grade A human being. That I came to think the same of Larry, Scherry, and Dick made it unanimous. Despite the fact that Al and I were most recently lowly prep siders, the three exalted ones were quick to treat us as equals. Dick's was what then referred to as "a delayed vocation," a polite term that didn't deter me from calling him "Ancient Age," which borrowed from but didn't allude to the bourbon of the same name. I can't imagine what I did or said to be baptized "the beast," a nickname that Scherry laid on me. Now that I think about it, however, I bet it was one of those ironic monikers that emphasize the opposite of one's characteristics, like calling a great big fellow "Tiny." Yeah, I'm pretty sure that's it.

One thing amused four of us and mystified the fifth. We ate lunch in UA's cafeteria, and all but Larry had seen more than once that he had a doppelganger on campus. Had you seen the guy, you'd have sworn he was Larry's identical twin. That he had never come to Larry's attention was made even more absurd when the four of us were already seated, eating at the same table, and Larry had just gotten into the cafeteria line. Guess who was right in front of him? Right! Finally, Larry would see him. The cafeteria line was open at both ends, with a wall in the middle, so when the twin, tray in hand, exited first, with Larry, tray in hand, not two steps behind him, it looked like a conveyor belt spitting out Larry Frederick Dolls. We were laughing the entire time he was making his way across the cafeteria to where we sat. "What's so funny?" he wanted to know. Yes, Larry managed to follow the man through the line and out the door without ever seeing him. I don't know if he ever did.

Our last night in Fayetteville wasn't what I would have expected in early June. That the summer session had concluded was a happy event, of course, and we celebrated that fact at supper and afterward, but my awareness that the five of us had no guarantee that we'd ever be together again was a solemn thought. And, as it happened, we never were.

FIDEM SCIT

IV • PHILOSOPHY

The two years our class spent studying the subject of philosophy, which amounted to our junior and senior years of college, run together in my mind for various reasons, and because of that I'm going to treat them together, trying not to create chronological contradiction or confusion as I go.

The most obvious change in living conditions moving from prep side to the upper side was that we went from dorm living to having a roommate. And mine, because I'm Irish and have a greater share of good luck than those not so fortunate, was my pal since fourth grade, Michael Charles O'Malley (I would have added his confirmation name, too, except he doesn't remember it—"Bartholomew?" he once haltingly suggested).

I told Mike that since he was younger and more agile, he should take the upper of the two bunks; my congenial friend agreed. It wasn't the first or last time that my blarney worked on him, though since he's been to Ireland and has kissed the famous stone, I dare not try it any more.

Mike and I were housed on the top floor of Morris Hall, with a window that faced south and looked out over the oval and the grounds all the way to the front gate. Our immediate neighbor to the east, in a room for one because he was a deacon, and rank at St. John's had its privileges, was Joe Orsini, a smart, funny, friendly fellow from New Jersey. Across the hall were Al and his roommate, L.D., whom I probably shouldn't always label as the liquor-bottle tosser, so I won't, this time. David Mikeska and Charlie Lipsmeyer were next door to Al and his roommate.

To say that I was a corrupting influence on Mike would be overstating it—a bit. One of the verboten possessions for seminarians, as you know, was a radio. But I found the idea of a small, unobtrusive transistor radio innocuous—one that could be heard only when a small earbud was plugged in, thereby not disturbing one's roommate. With a radio, I could keep up-to-date about news, weather, and any national disaster that was pending. Maybe, from time to time, I might listen to a bit of popular music (so as not to get out of touch with modern trends), and, in my spare time when I didn't need to study, I could catch an inning or two of the Cardinals or possibly some football or basketball games in season.

To say further that I developed some rationalizing talents whilst in the sem is something with which I won't argue. But why study philosophy if one can't exercise some original thinking of one's own? So, getting back to the subject of corruption of my roommate, I have to say that somehow Mike got wind of or intuited that I had asked that our seminary store, which had a catalogue from which we could order a variety of goods, to purchase a transistor for me. I think I paid about $8.00 for it (a high-end selection), including the postage.

Mike asked me if I had ordered a radio. "I ordered a diode," I told him. I had seen that word in the information in the catalogue. It apparently was part of the electronic circuitry. When Mike asked the same question again, and I gave the same answer, he dropped the subject.

When the radio arrived, I obviously couldn't and didn't try to conceal the fact that I was listening to it from time to time. He never asked to listen. He was trying to obey the seminary rule. Had he said to me, "Get thee behind me, Radio Satan," it would have been appropriate.

It was basketball season when I found, unexpectedly, that I could pick up a Chicago station. Two or three nights a week it was broadcasting the games of Loyola University of Chicago, once a little-known team, but in March of 1963 it shocked the country by winning the N.C.A.A. national championship. Being a provincial sort of guy, I was thrilled that a Catholic university had won the tournament, so I eagerly tuned in to the Ramblers' broadcasts in the fall of '63 into 1964.

Mike knew what I was hearing, and he tried mightily to resist the temptation to listen. I'd be sitting on my bottom bunk or at my desk and was apparently voicing either enthusiasm for what had just happened on the court or my unhappiness about it. I swear that I wasn't trying to rope Mike in. One night, however, he had had enough. I felt a tap on the shoulder.

"Let me hear it, too." So ended Mike's admirable holdout, and thus began my bad influence.

Had Mike O'Malley's surname have been different, perhaps he'd have been assigned someone else for a roommate, as several of the first year fellows on the upper side seem to have been paired up alphabetically. But get me, he did, and I have to confess that heavier over my head than inducing him to listen to basketball games hangs the fact that one too many times I offered him a Lucky Strike. In my rationalized defense I plead that in the fall of '63 there was no surgeon general's report on the dangers of smoking, though it was common knowledge among virtually all of us who took up the habit, that smoking detracted from one's "wind," as athletes of that time put it.

So Mike eventually had a Lucky Strike (unfiltered) or two, and before long he was buying his own smokes. I would be feeling worse at this remove from my introduction of Mike to Lucky Strike but for the fact that he has not smoked for many years. If he were still puffing away, I would feel bad about it—deservedly so.

*

Among the deacons that year was a fellow from Lafayette, Louisiana who was proudly, profoundly southern. Though I had been apprised of this allegiance, I had forgotten it when, on an errand to his room, I saw a clear glass jar on his bookshelf with something dark within. When asked what was in the jar, he said, "Soil from the Holy Land." Seeing my surprise, he added the punch line: "Richmond."

*

pre-1961: Do you remember the story of Monsignor Aretz and the library books scattered on the floor? This is a tale I heard about the same room in which those events supposedly occurred. I was told this by one who witnessed, according to him, what follows:

The witness was a young man I had known since grade school; he had a brother who was a deacon. It was the summer before the deacon would be ordained a priest the following May, and he was living at and working at St. John's. The deacon's bed was located in what had once been the library but had been converted to a dormitory. He invited his younger brother, in Little Rock for a visit, to spend a night or two with him at the seminary. The dorm had lots of vacant beds, as only a couple of seminarians were staying there over the summer.

The brother reported to me that on one night only he and his brother were sleeping in the dorm. The moon was bright, and visibility in the dorm was as good as one could expect in a room with no lights on. Sometime in the early hours of morning both were awakened by odd sounds. Then it became clear to them both what they were hearing: The blinds in two of the several windows were going up and down. They did it several times and then stopped. No visible agent was the cause. The room in which Monsignor Aretz, years before, might have witnessed something bizarre was the location of another such event.

*

The game of touch football at St. John's was suddenly no more. Flag football had replaced it. In touch football as it was played at St. John's, in order for a runner to be "downed," his forward progress halted, a defender had to touch him with both hands. Disputes sometimes arose when there was a difference of opinion as to whether that had taken place. Well, flag football put an end to that.

In flag, each player had a belt to which, at the hips, were attached red strips of fiber, perhaps two feet long—the "flags." They could be attached to the hip belt (with Velcro?) and easily yanked off by a defensive player. Arguments about whether a man was down had ceased. It was during such a game that on the team opposite me was a fellow not often seen in intramurals. Only by stretching to its breaking point the definition of *athlete* would this player be included.

He was skinny; he was slow; he was uncoordinated; his eyesight was poor. Have I made my point? OK, so he was no jock. The fact that he wanted to play was all that was needed for all the participants to say, "Welcome," even if the team of which he was a member couldn't count on him to add to its chances of winning. In touch and flag football, somebody has to center the ball to the quarterback, even though it means he's delayed running out for passes. Centers don't get to catch passes often—or ever.

This guy, call him Les, was the center. I was defending against his team when Les, slow though he was, became his quarterback's last option. He threw the pass to Les, who caught it! If you've ever seen a non-football player try to run with the ball, his lack of experience shows immediately as he grasps it: He puts his entire arm around the ball with its pointed tips directed to the sky and the ground simultaneously.

Thus did Les cradle the old pigskin after he managed to hold on to the pass. I was the only defender near him, so unlikely was it that he needed to be covered. As I loped over to grab his red flag, Les broke into his version of a trot—you couldn't call it a run. I remember being amused by Les's ungainly gait as I approached. Herky-jerky and seemingly going in three directions at once, Les was about to have his flag yanked from his belt.

I'm sure you can see where this is going: Yep, Les's flag zigged when on any ordinary runner it would have zagged. And I went for the anticipated zag and completely missed. Thrown off balance by my failure to snatch his flag, I stumbled, then fell. And from that front row seat (of my pants) I saw Les "run" until he crossed the goal line. His teammates (and mine!) were simultaneously celebrating Les's TD and alerting any bystanders who might have missed the play of my disastrous attempt to cover him. When one's own teammates are cooperating with the opposition to ridicule one's efforts, one knows that his athletic reputation is going down a notch or two.

By suppertime that night, even those seminarians whose interest in flag football was at the same level as their desire to be poked in the eye with a blunt stick were aware of Les's feat and my clumsy feet. Life is sometimes a humility sandwich, and every day, for a while, I took another bite.

*

Another unhappy development occurred some weeks later just a few yards from where Les "faked me out of my jock," as we used to say. Prior to yet another intramural gridiron classic, I and a couple of teammates were warming up by tossing passes back and forth. A fellow from Pine Bluff, fast and with good hands, was one of those involved. Ball in hand, I signaled for him to take off, planning to throw him a long one. Knowing of his speed, I threw the ball about as far as I could, realizing too late that my pass was offline, and both the ball and my intended receiver were heading for a tall, fully grown pine tree. Despite my shout of his name, hoping that would stop or slow him, on he ran, colliding with the tree just as he was about to make the catch.

Knocked out, prostrate, unmoving, the would-be receiver was a ghastly sight as I ran to him. I was grateful when he began to move one of his legs as I and the third fellow stood over him. Eventually he regained consciousness, and as we helped him to his feet I was surprised to hear #3 say, "Are you gonna be able to play today, Bob?" He wasn't. The swollen side of his head was visible for at least a couple of days, and the black eye lasted even longer. That end of the upper side football field holds no warm memories for me.

*

When we prep siders went to the upper side for the last two years of college, we were joined in the class by new seminarians who transferred from what were termed "minor" seminaries (four years of high school and two of college) that were located in dioceses outside Arkansas. Maybe I was wrong in my judgment at the time, but it seemed to me that some of the lads from north of the Mason-Dixon Line weren't exactly thrilled to be in Little Rock among the hicks and hillbillies.

I base some of this thinking on an incident that grew out of a class we took: Logic. Thinking logically is probably a goal of most humans, so any kind of class that would promote that would be beneficial. In the first weeks we learned about things such as syllogisms, which are step-by-step methods of reaching conclusions, and logical fallacies, arguments that may seem valid but whose foundations are shaky.

I remember that one night's homework had to do with figuring out textbook questions that looked like riddles, but whose answers could be arrived at by, (what else!) logical thinking. One problem was especially thorny. If we had been in possession of computers that night, and had the Internet existed, we could have readily found the answer. It's a well known exercise in logic, and variations of it are common online these days.

The problem had to do with a jailer and three prisoners. The jailer offered to free them all if one of them could guess correctly what color hat the jailer had placed on his head; each was blindfolded until all were wearing a hat. If they failed to make a correct guess, they would have their sentence doubled (or they would be shot, or fed to lions, or worse, depending on the version one encounters). There were x-number of red and x of white, and, according to the details of the logic problem, two of the prisoners couldn't guess their own hat, but the third guy could, and he was blind! So, how did he do it?

As Mike and I, looking at our logic homework that night, began to tussle with that problem, it soon became apparent that it was defying our attempts to be logical. Other confounded students took to the hall, seeking out someone who had the answer. A couple of those answer-seekers were sent from the corridor where the new guys lived. Apparently no one on their wing had the key to the problem, either. I wondered if they were there to assure themselves that nobody in the class could figure it out.

One pair of roommates hadn't joined the semi-throng racking its collective brains in the hall. Al Schneider and his roommate's door was closed. Somebody said, "Go ask Al," (who is a native Arkie – from Nettleton, a small town in northeast part of state). Being in the mix of those in the hall trying to unlock the riddle, I heard a comment from one of the interlopers that asking was "a waste of time."

Somebody did ask Al. When the questioner turned and said to us, "He's got it!" I don't know if there was more happiness or disbelief among those of us in the hall. We gathered at the door to Al's room, and quietly and logically, as was and is his wont, he explained it all.

When the newcomers took off to their hall with the answer to the riddle, an answer unexpectedly supplied by an Arkie, I took pleasure in thinking that Al, singlehandedly, might have put a crack in a stereotype.

P.S. If you want details about and a solution to the puzzle, Wikipedia has it all under the heading "Prisoners and Hats Puzzle."

*

There's one thing I want to add about the fellow who went to Al's door. An ironclad custom dictated that he NOT knock! He was to scratch on the door. That was the signal that it was a fellow student outside the door. If a priest came to a student's door, he would knock; it was the universal way to identify one's standing to the residents inside.

Further, one day while traipsing past a priest's apartment, I saw one of his brother priests at his door—scratching.

*

When another priest didn't show up to teach a high school class one day, Father Drane, who didn't teach at that level, noticed the other priest's absence and decided to teach tenth graders some philosophy. I knew that happened because I was chatting with one of the wise fools that afternoon, and he was proudly telling me that he had been taught some philosophy that day.

"What did Father Drane teach you?"

"He taught us about a man named Couldnt."

It took me a moment to analyze the statement. "Do you think it might have been Kant?"

"Yeah. That was him."

*

Visiting Little Rock was James Pike, a high-profile Episcopalian bishop who was considered ultra-liberal by some for his views on racial and gender injustice, just to mention two of many issues. Bishop Pike had been a Catholic as a boy, but transferred his allegiance in adulthood. Whatever he was doing in Little Rock, I'm sure that coming to St. John's to give a speech wasn't on his schedule until he crossed paths in downtown with two of our deacons. Monsignor O'Connell, our rector, was gone from St. John's that day, and that, coupled with the spirit of ecumenism that was prevalent in those days, might have emboldened the deacons to invite the bishop to come to St. John's to address their brother seminarians. And come he did.

A hastily arranged speech was delivered to the major seminarians who chose to attend. It took place in late afternoon. When word of the speech was published in the newspaper shortly thereafter (perhaps the next day) fireworks were ignited. I can't name a single circumstance of anyone's being reprimanded or penalized for the event, nor do I know that the bishop said anything scandalous when he talked to the seminarians. But a good deal of heat, if not light, was generated by the impulsive invitation.

What did I think of the speech? Well, you might recall I mentioned that attendance was voluntary. It seems that roommate Mike and I were engaged in a bit of one-on-one on the basketball court behind the refectory that afternoon, and even though we knew that the bell that rang at 4:30 was calling all interested parties to the event, it seems that we were tied in our match-up and had already decided that the winner had to win by two baskets; so, of course we *had* to play on—which, as it turned out, was all the way through the good bishop's lecture. And, no, neither of us can remember who won.

*

I mean no disrespect to Monsignor O'Connell (with whom I felt a bond, since his surname was my mother's maiden name), but logical story-telling requires that I mention that his absence from St. John's the day of Bishop Pike's appearance wasn't an entirely uncommon situation. I can't say that I was ever aware of any extended periods when he was not present at the seminary, but it's possible that at an earlier time in his career as rector he may have been so. I did hear that he was fast friends with a Little Rock family with whom he spent time.

Anyway, I have to report that because of his real or imagined absences, Monsignor O'Connell was dubbed with a nickname, a name that older Catholics will immediately recognize as the title of a nationally distributed Catholic newspaper: *Our Sunday Visitor.*

*

pre-1961: Father John Doyle, one of the Little Rock diocese's gifts from Pennsylvania, and one of my favorite teachers at Catholic High, told me about the night before his ordination to the priesthood.

For Catholics the most solemn moments of the Mass occur at the consecration, when the priest's words, taken from those said by Jesus at the Last Supper, miraculously turn the bread and wine into the body and blood of Christ. After saying in Latin, "For this is my body," John Doyle would, at his first Mass as celebrant, raise the consecrated host for all present to see, a demonstration emphasized by the altar boy's ringing of a small, hand-held bell.

That night in May, sometime in the 1940s, he went to bed for the last time as a deacon. One can only guess at his excitement and anticipation as a goal sought over years of intense study was about to be reached. Far into the night, after much tossing and turning, he finally fell into a fitful sleep, sleep that was interrupted by a sound.

Alone in his deacon's quarters, John sat up, confused by what he heard. Then he recognized it for what it was: the sound of the bell that was rung at the consecration. He was alternately amazed and uneasy. Was this audible visitation real? Was he hallucinating? The bell would sound thrice, just as it did at Mass, then stop. Then it would ring again. He determined that it came from outside his open widow. The springtime air carried it into his room. He went to the window after switching on the light in his room.

Then he saw the bell, on a string, that went perpendicularly to the room above his, the room occupied by John's friend Tex Vogel, a known joker. One can only surmise that the DNA of St. John's must always have included the trait that anyone and everyone could be a target of a prank—any time, any place.

*

I can't recall how it ever occurred to more than one of us that a trip to New Orleans over what is now called Spring Break was possible, much less a good idea. But somehow it worked out that three of us, Charlie Lipsmeyer, Bill Cingolani, and I set off from St. John's in a car that Father Benz loaned us, a vintage Ford that had very few miles on it for its age and was in excellent condition. If I had to guess, I'd say Bill (a.k.a. Cing) probably brought up the subject of the auto loan to Father Benz. Cing was an outgoing, friendly lad with the gift of gab, so he likely produced the unlikely car for us to take. Our fourth partner in the adventure was to be Dave Mikeska, Charlie's roommate, and he had gone home to Longview, Texas right as the Break began, so we would dip into the Lone Star state and get him on our way to NOLA, as it's commonly called these days.

Following our plan (perhaps too grand a word to use), we all brought along approximately the same amount of money. "All for one, and one for all" was our motto. We were going to vote on every proposed expenditure, needing three votes to bring about any spending. The first leg of our journey was to McGehee, Cing's home town in southeast Arkansas, where we ate in a restaurant that may have been his family's. Travel, all agree, is a great educator, and as Cing explained to me the contents of the entrees identified as "Mountain Oysters" and "Turkey Fries," I realized that wasn't yet out of Arkansas and was having my culinary horizon vastly broadened.

Into Texas and to Longview we went, spending the night with Dave's most gracious parents and congenial siblings. Then the quartet was off to our Louisiana destination. My sister Luci and her husband Bob Hall lived in Metairie, a suburb of New Orleans, and they were nice enough to feed us fried chicken the night we got into town.

Our decision to vote on expenditures had repercussions that we hadn't anticipated. At restaurants, ordering food took longer than usual because each of us had to propose what he wanted to eat and get approval before letting the waitress know his choice. For me, the only smoker in the group, I had more than once to counter suggestions that I needed to cut back on my frequency of burning up the group's dough. I don't recall any real disputes, but the system was sometimes unwieldy.

One evening, after supper and some other time-burning activity which I don't recall, we were heading to our motel down a street with no other cars passing or trailing us. It was deserted but for a lone walker. He looked old and slow. And then he looked horizontal—face-first into the sidewalk! We stopped, got out, and as soon as we got to him we could smell the booze. He had been holding a package, which flew from his hands as he fell. One of us went to get it as we tried to help the fellow to his feet. We got him to a sitting position when the sound of a car coming at high speed was followed by another sound: screeching brakes.

From driver and passenger side quickly emerged two men, well dressed, probably in their 30s or 40s. Each held a long, lit flashlight which they were pointing in our faces as they yelled at us. The drift of their commands was to get away from the old man and to stand away—next to the wall of a building. They thought we had mugged the guy, and we insisted that we saw him fall, that he was drunk, and they would smell the alcohol if only they would get a whiff of him.

As one man went to the old-timer and the other was herding us to the wall, Charlie not only went to the wall as they hollered at us to do, but he turned to face it, spread his legs and extended his hands up against the wall, as if he were to be frisked. The man who was separating us from the drunk growled something to Charlie like, "You're not on TV; you don't have to do that."

Soon they reached the conclusion that the drunk *was* drunk and that we hadn't harmed him. The men told us they were volunteers who kept watch on their neighborhood. As we got back in our car, I, for one, was shaken by the encounter, and found it ironic that when one of the vigilantes discovered we were visiting New Orleans, he said, "Hope you enjoy your visit." Well, we had up until then.

The next day we were walking in downtown New Orleans on a street busy with both automotive and foot traffic. I saw a man lying on the sidewalk, next to a building, whether sleeping or drunk or dead, I don't know. But he was invisible to all those who walked past him. I suppose that my traveling companions saw him, too. With the lesson of the night before fresh in our minds, none of us made a move to see what was wrong. I say "wrong" because people don't as a rule, lie on concrete, unmoving, unless something is wrong. The moment I walked past him I felt guilty. To this day I regret my inaction.

On the way home, our four Musketeers approach to money matters was threatened by an unforeseen event: steam coming from the Ford's radiator. We were really near rock bottom as far as cash was concerned. Our food purchases had been cut back to a Coke and a cinnamon roll for breakfast, and we had what looked like just enough moolah to pay for our gas to get back to LR. I looked at the two remaining cigarettes in my pack and knew they would have to last. We must have been at least a hundred miles from Little Rock when we first noticed the steam; it was a jarring sight in the before-everybody-has-a-credit-card-with-him period of U.S. history.

We pulled into a gas station. Dave had an idea of how to deal with the leaking radiator. He took a couple of bucks from whoever was acting as treasurer that day and went into the office. He emerged with a product in his hand. Its label read, "STOP-LEAK." If ever I hoped for truth in advertising, it was then. Allowing the car to cool for a while, we watched hopefully as Dave unscrewed the radiator cap, his hand covered with a rag he borrowed from somebody in the service station. Eventually the steam emerging from the radiator stopped, and he poured the contents of the vial and some water into it. We got back in the car, with Dave at the wheel, as if he was taking full responsibility for getting us back home. Within a few miles the steam stopped, and we declared Dave an automotive genius.

The trip had been educational; we learned some things about New Orleans and ourselves—not all of it good.

*

A scream at two in the morning is hard to imagine as a good thing. So when Mike and I heard one, we both assumed something terrible had happened, and it sounded like the source of the throaty vibrations was right outside our door. So, brave lads that we were, we asked each other, "What was that?" When we had decided after a unanimous vote that we had heard what we had heard, we opened our door—a crack.

There, in the hall stood a stunned, shaken Charlie Lips-meyer, from just across the hall. He was standing at the door of our next door neighbor, Joe Orsini, the deacon. So we looked that way as well. Standing in the doorway was none other than the resident himself, not looking too swell either.

Joe was the infirmarian for at least our floor, if not for all of the upper side. *Infirmarian* is probably a bit grander title than the job itself, which consisted mainly of handing out pills, usually for headaches and upset stomachs. But when one was headachy or sick to his stomach and had no relief at hand, the infirmarian was someone that we were glad was available. It was for that reason—an acute bellyache— that Charlie was scratching at Joe's door at what was exactly the middle of the night (lights out: 10:00 P.M., morning wake-up bell: 6:00 a.m.).

Joe, it turned out, was the screamer. The reason for his vocal outburst he explained in an honest confession, delivered on the spot. Joe screamed because a dead priest was, at that moment, two floors below, resting in the chapel with seminarians keeping watch over coffin and corpse. Joe said that being in the same building with a dead person was just not something with which he was comfortable. When he heard Charlie moaning,

"Joe! Joe!" at his door, his subconscious went into overdrive, and it shook him up enough that he let fly with his New Jersey version of the Rebel Yell.

By the time Joe had explained the cause of his outburst, others living on our hall had apparently had nerve enough to investigate, and they gathered for another explanation; by then Joe had apologized for at least the second time for frightening any and all within earshot, especially Charlie, whom he escorted to wherever it was that the Pepto-Bismol was stored.

*

Since I've just mentioned the issue of a post-midnight scream, it's fitting to mention the other. This one came from the opposite wing of our floor. It originated in a room that was down our hall, then left on the main corridor of the building, and around the corner. I would guesstimate the distance to be maybe 150 feet from our room. Despite that, it was plenty loud enough to awaken Mike and me. We and our corridor mates went to investigate, as did virtually everyone on the floor. By the time we got close to the room from which the yelling came, the hallway was blocked with inquiring (nosy?) seminarians. An explanation drifted back through the crowd: bad dream; screamer is fine; has no idea of what set off the yell; roommate not quite fine just yet. End of story.

But virtually from the next day the fellow whose nightmare shook up the floor started to experience hair loss. Small patches of the hair on his head were the first sign of the process, which, unfortunately, continued until I heard he had lost all hair—all. He soldiered on, gamely suffering through what for some of us would have been an embarrassing experience. A priest with the same name as the screamer, and located in the diocese for which he was studying is pictured on the Internet, so I'm convinced that he achieved his career goal, despite what, if it had happened to me, would have been a real obstacle.

*

Another strange nighttime happening: As I was settling down after lights out to go to sleep, I saw something very odd. Lights seemed to be dancing on my pillow as I adjusted it for maximum comfort. Knowing that Mike, in the bunk above mine was likely not asleep, I broke Grand Silence and asked him to look at the strange lights. He bent over from above to see what I was talking about. At that point, wouldn't you know it, as I leaned away from the pillow for him to see, the lights went out. He reported, as I knew he would, that he saw nothing. "What the heck was that?" I wondered as I fell asleep.

A couple of nights later, the weirdness continued: same pattern, same time, same lights, and same lack of them when my roomie took a look. Not being accustomed to visual hallucinations, I really was more than a little disturbed by the appearance of flashing emanations from my pillow that disappeared when a witness was called on to see them.

Then one night I figured it all out: as I manipulated my pillow shortly after getting into bed, I saw that static electricity that I had built up by walking on the rug by our bunk beds was reacting with the plastic cover that I had on my pillow, a dust cover that was located between the pillow and the pillowcase. "Mike! Look!" As my roomie, more than a little weary of being asked to witness the invisible, peered down from above, I said, manipulating the pillow, "See the lights? They appear everywhere my fingers touch the pillow. It's static electricity that's making the sparks. You see them, don't you?"

"I see them," he said, not altogether convincingly. Asked again for a bit more conviction in his voice, Mike said, "I see them!" To this day, when asked to validate my visions, he responds with palpable irony, "Oh, yeah, sure, I saw them."

*

Father Drane got his Ph.D. in philosophy from the University of Madrid. He was excited to announce to those of us in philosophy that a favorite professor from U of M was going to visit him and would give us a talk. We "philosophers" gathered to hear the man, a small, elderly fellow with a decided accent but whose English was excellent. Our meeting place was a lounge in Fletcher Hall, the newest building on campus, named for Bishop Albert Fletcher.

Father Drane took great pleasure in introducing his former mentor, and the professor was obviously fond of his outgoing former student. Behind the professor was a portable greenboard (high-tech at the time!) and the teacher was soon, chalk in hand, writing vigorously thereon.

What happened next I attribute to a distraction of some kind that briefly altered Father Drane's concentration on what the professor was saying. He was discussing insincere pious language and wrote a synonym for that idea on the board: *cant*. While *cant* isn't a common word, I saw nodding heads as he discussed it, so it wasn't an entirely unknown choice to his audience. That's when Father Drane saw the word on the board. He was sitting off to the side of and slightly behind the professor. He rose and went to the board without being seen by our speaker. Father Drane held his left index finger to his lips, letting us know not to alert the speaker of what he was about to do. He got the chalk and added an apostrophe to *cant*.

But he was caught in the act by him who had knowingly written the word without the apostrophe. "No, no, no!" he said to his protégé. Father Drane assured him that the apostrophe was indeed required. Back and forth they went, with the professor getting just a mite agitated at his student who was insisting that he was right. Finally the professor shrugged his shoulders and returned to his speech. Afterwards someone may have informed Father Drane of his error, but being just a fledging "philosopher," I didn't.

*

I told you of the teacher who put one of my classmates into a near-comatose state by reading from the textbook. There was at least one other teacher-reader on the faculty, and the soporific power of his words were said to be virtually universal in their effect. He didn't notice when he induced sleep, I was told, because he NEVER looked up from his text. Eventually he and I crossed paths in the classroom, and his don't-look-up rule was put to the test.

I sat several rows back and was trying to fight off Morpheus when I saw a black cat walk across the front of the room, not four feet from where the teacher stood (he ALWAYS stood).

He took no notice of the feline, not then when it passed, nor when it jumped up onto the seat of a desk in the front row, also only a few feet from the teacher. There was but one other occupant of the front row, a Louisiana lad by the name of Frank Chalaire. Frank was the diligent type, and I'd guess he was front and center in the hope that his proximity to the teacher would keep him awake.

From my perch (graduated rows of desks) near the back of the room, I was totally awake as a small but diverting drama was playing out. The threesome, teacher, student, and cat, were within six feet of each other. Frank stared at the cat, located on a desk between him and the teacher, and the cat stared back at Frank, and the teacher stared at his book.

Those who had fallen asleep were nudged to consciousness by the awake, and soon the entire class was staring, too. The sight of the four eyeballs (two human, two feline) in the front row fastened on each other was killing! Stifled laughter was contagious, but it DIDN'T interrupt the recitation. Who would win the staring contest, Frank or the cat? Would, for ONCE the teacher acknowledge that something other than his textbook was present in the classroom?

The answers: Frank and no. The cat eventually got stared down and left as he had entered. The book's power held sway on the reader, but all of us were still awake when the bell rang.

*

From time to time during our meals we had spiritual reading as an accompaniment. This is an almost daily practice at some religious institutions and was mentioned earlier in conjunction with the priests' retreat. Its use at our seminary was sporadic. At any rate, when it was time for such reading at meals, we who were eating were expected to listen quietly while one of us read from a book whose contents were either morally uplifting or practically applicable to the life of a priest. It fell to us in first philosophy, since we were in our first year on the upper side, to do the reading. Readers were taken from an alphabetical list. The hams among us probably enjoyed the duty, but for some others public reading is close to public speaking as one of humanity's worst fears.

One night when reading was to occur, all the food had been distributed and a bell was rung, signaling the start of the reading. The voice that we heard was so strained that it almost sounded as if it were emanating from the throat of a person being strangled. The young man from whose throat the words were being squeezed was new to St. John's that year, and my impression of him had been that he was a bright, outgoing sort.

But a quick glance in his direction, a glance that many in the room were taking, showed a person whose reading duty was putting a terrible strain on him. His body was bent, as if a hundred pounds had been placed on his shoulders, as he battled to force the words on the page to be heard. To his credit he struggled on, and we who had turned to see him quickly turned away lest our ogling add to his burden. A young man who would attempt to follow a vocation that surely would present him with such a monumental task as overcoming that fear was a person to be admired. He reminded me of a deacon of a few years before, whose stutter as he delivered a sermon at Mass signaled a huge challenge for his priesthood. The deacon was ordained but left the priesthood less than a year later. Whether the reader that night became a priest, I can't say.

*

I don't know why I decided to volunteer for furnace duty; it may have had to do with the fact that Larry Frederick, with whom I spent the summer at the U of A in Fayetteville, was the chief of the crew, and I admired him for it. Why admire him or the other furnace crew members? Because they had to get up at four o'clock on the coldest mornings of the year and hike perhaps 75 yards from the main building to the power house and turn on the gas furnace that heated the boilers that sent steam heat to all the other buildings—that's why.

When Larry sent out word that he needed another member of the crew (each member took one week's duty at a time), I told him I was his man (boy?). He turned me over to George Radosovich, the second in command, for my instruction. One of the nicest fellows I ever knew at St. John's, George was a patient teacher who led me through the steps involved in getting heat to the masses—and the Masses.

The power house was notable for a tall smokestack that emerged from its roof, perhaps to eliminate the fumes from the gas burners within. So there we were, George and I, kneeling at the hinged metal door that, when opened, revealed a huge boiler, presumably filled with water that had to be heated so steam could create warmth.

The first tool I was shown resembled a straightened coat hanger—for Paul Bunyan's jacket. It was about five feet long, and at its end was a slot that held a short candle. When lit, the candle could ignite a pilot light, which George demonstrated. A small lever was depressed to bring gas to the pilot light. He had me light the pilot and then turn it off a time or two. Got it! Light the pilot.

Once the pilot was on, the furnace itself, long rows of gas-filled tubes, had to be fired. George showed me the lever that would send gas to those tubes. It was about the length and size of a baseball bat. When George lifted the lever, the flames burst into being, with a "whoomp" that surprised me. Why, I asked George, did he turn his back to the furnace when he lifted the lever? "That's so, if the furnace blows up, it won't get you in the face."

Despite that, I became a crew member. It was our duty to rise at four and to use the official furnace crew flashlight to look out our window at the official furnace crew thermometer that was affixed to the inside of the screen on the window; that inspection of the thermometer was to see if the temperature that morning was below 40 degrees. That's right, *below* 40. Only then was one to go light the furnace.

We who were on the crew had a surprisingly high profile because we were lobbied by many of our brethren to ignore the official turn-on number of sub- 40 and give everybody who was cold-natured a break and, instead, use 50 as our guide. I used to joke with those who urged me to fudge the numbers by telling them that I used my cigarette lighter to consult the thermometer rather than the flashlight. "That's no good!" the credulous among them would protest. "You'll never turn on the heat if you do it that way!"

I had two surprises doing furnace duty. On my first morning, as I put the key into the lock, my flashlight exposed on the power house door, I heard a strange, muffled, sort of scratchy sound. When I entered and turned on the lights, I couldn't account for it. All was quiet within. When I saw Larry later that day, I asked him if he ever heard that noise. "Yes," he said laughing, "it's just the rats." Rats? Enough to make a sound like that come through a door? "Don't worry," he said. "You'll never see them. They won't come out until you turn off the lights and leave." That made me feel *much* better!

The second surprise had to do with one morning on my return trip from the power house to Morris Hall where all of us on the upper side lived. As I walked from the power house, I looked up and saw that every room on that side of the building had its lights on! There must have been at least two dozen rooms on that side of the building. What was going on that every room would have its lights on before 4:30 in the morning? And why, I suddenly noticed, were all the lights silver? I thought I was hallucinating. Have you seen in movies how people who can't believe what they are seeing rub their eyes, as if to rub away some strange sight? Well, I did that. And it didn't work. All the silver lights were still on. I turned my back on the windows, thinking to refocus my eyes. That's when I saw the full, silvery moon behind me.

*

The worst day at St. John's in my time there was the day that Charlie Fischer died. Charlie and a couple other guys were swimming in the Arkansas River when an undertow got him. My clearest memory of Charlie is his ever-present smile. We lost a very good young man that day.

∗

From the serious to the silly, I recall the day that our two best softball pitchers were facing off, and the hits were hard to come by. Both Illinois lads, the hurlers were Bob Fellner and Bob Hasenstab. Having played baseball as a kid, I never faced pitchers throwing overhand (from a greater distance than in softball, it is true) who were as fast as these two underhanded slingers. Both used the windmill windup and delivery that characterize what is often called "fast-pitch" softball (as opposed to the lazy, high arcing toss used in "slow pitch").

Bob Hasenstab was really on that day, striking out our side inning after inning. I had already whiffed twice when I virtually closed my eyes as I swung on the first pitch of my third at-bat and somehow hit the ball—over the left field fence! Bob just grinned as I stood at home, astounded, as the ball went beyond the short left field barrier. He waved his glove at me, telling me to round the bases, both of us acutely aware of how the luck of the Irish had just made a visit to the diamond.

∗

pre-1961: Not long after I got to the sem, I saw an elderly man walking a dog across the oval, both heading for the refectory. I learned that he was Joe Kleuser, the long-time handyman who lived in an apartment attached to the back of the gymnasium. Joe must have been in his eighties when I first became aware of him, but he was often out walking his dog, which, Al tells me, may have been named

Schmalz. It was a tiny hound, but even so, such a determined pull-er-on-the-leash it was, that when the twosome were seen circling the oval, the usual observation was, "The dog is out walking Joe." When one would greet Joe, who was apparently hard of hearing (not a bad thing for one who had to live so close to the basketball goings-on in the gym), he would reply to virtually any salutation (from "How's it going, Joe?" to "Nice day, isn't it?") with a resounding, "How!" I once got a glimpse of Joe's small workshop that was in the basement area of the gym, a tiny room crammed with mountains of screws, tools, and every other gizmo that a handyman might accrue over the years. My mind boggles at the chore that was involved in cleaning out the space after Joe's passing.

*

Two enterprising young fellows decided, after a fortuitous discovery, to give the seminary a concert. Adventurers both, they verified the rumor that there was a way to get on the roof of Morris hall. When they ascended to the top, they discovered two loudspeakers there. I have no answer for the "why?" and the "when?" of the speakers' existence. But unused speakers, it seemed to the two, were a waste. So they managed to run a couple very long wires from their room to the roof. The wires were attached to an item that was verboten but nonetheless present in their room: a record player.

When the hookup was complete, they fired up the phonograph, and timing its output to a period when lots of seminarians were out on the grounds, they slid a piece of classical music (a rousing number, possibly Wagner's "Ride of the Valkyries") on the turntable and dropped the arm on the first groove of the record.

The broadcast music was astounding not only for its mere existence but also for its volume, as I'm sure it carried far beyond the seminary boundaries. The purveyors knew that their creation was to have a short life, as sooner rather than later the authorities would call for an investigation of who and how. So after the first selection came to an end, the music makers yanked the wires that they had attached (but not too tightly) to the speakers, and they reeled them in, no trace of their transmission of music to the roof left to be found. The caper's creators became folk heroes to those who found out their identities, and as far as I know they were never revealed to the rector or anyone else who might have called for their prosecution.

If you saw a scene in "The Shawshank Redemption" that reminds you of this incident, to give credit where it's due, I mention that the St. John's event preceded Stephen King's short story by 20 years and the movie by ten more.

*

As if being roommates for 180 days of the school year were not enough, Mike and I decided to take a trip to the New York World's Fair in the summer of 1964. We got our Greyhound round-trip tickets and boarded for a journey that would take virtually an entire day. Highlights along the way included a bathroom stall peeper, a bus so crowded that we stood for what seemed like a long time, having given our seats to a couple of women (one with a child) whose inclusion among the passengers by the driver went beyond the maximum seating capacity.

The women felt guilty, I guess, after a couple hours of watching us stand, and she who had an infant and the other woman volunteered their seats to us, the mother asking me to hold her child. Happy for what I thought of as a ten-minute break, I accepted, not anticipating that junior would pick the time I was holding him to empty his bladder.

Oh well, just twenty-plus hours after leaving LR, we were in NY. In 1964 we had no access to TripAdvisor to scout out the best of the economical hotels in Gotham; we had no smart phone to guide us to our destination nor to send a signal to Uber that we needed transportation; we had no credit card to meet unanticipated expenses. I know what you're thinking: "A modern-day Lewis and Clark!" How right you are.

So there we were, in the New York Greyhound bus station with no place to stay the night, and after that bus ride we could really use a nap! So I withdrew a dime from my pocket and called a hotel (found in the Yellow pages—yet another indication of the primitive conditions at the time)) without having the slightest idea of where it was, what it would cost per night, and what its amenities were. Imagine my surprise when I asked the desk clerk if the hotel had a room with a double bed and he said, "Yes." He told me the price per day. It was in our range. I said that we'd take it.

"That's Mr. and Mrs. who?" he inquired. Not a married couple I explained, two college boys. "Buddy," he snarled accusatorily, "that's illegal for two guys to share the same bed!" I immediately felt guilty and ignorant. Imagine that! A dumb ole Arkie wanting to enter into such a disgusting arrangement. I had the presence of mind, despite my shame, to ask if two single beds were available and was told they were not.

I got the same message several times again, with me reporting to Mike, standing outside the phone booth guarding our bags, that finding accommodations in the midst of a World's Fair was proving harder than we anticipated. Then I struck pay dirt: the George Washington Hotel had what we needed at a reasonable price. Hooray!

Somehow we figured out the route to the Lexington Avenue location of the hotel and took a bus there, of course. Our second "Welcome to New York" moment took place on that bus ride as a worker from the garment district, pushing one of those stereotypical, wheeled garment racks, took exception to something our driver did and twice used his rack as a battering ram on the side of the bus where we were sitting and, as he did so, offered an opinion about the driver's legitimacy. We were definitely in the big city now.

On our arrival at the hotel, wanting to make sure that our stay there would not be interrupted by new arrivals, we paid for several days in advance, four as I recall. Our room for two at the G.W. was a marvel: somehow, a tiny room for one had had a second bed squeezed into it. No, the two beds were not a double bed, which would be "illegal," but the fact that they were pushed up against each other made the distinction between a double and a single hard to see. The bathroom was tiny, and the shower was one in which a revolution of the torso during the laving was hard to achieve. But we had a room, and it was the Fair, not the hotel that we had come to New York to see.

It was a Friday afternoon that we arrived, and if you're wondering how I can recall that, I can do so because our first night of dining had to exclude a certain entrée: meat. The Catholic abstention from animal flesh was not a problem for me as I saw a favorite on the menu, French toast. When the waiter came, I ordered it as it was presented on the menu, *pain perdu*, my French accent probably not great, but one I thought reasonable. He gave me a disgusted look, one that suggested disapproval of my attempt to be, however briefly, bi-lingual. "Do you mean French toast?" he said, perhaps a purist offended by my failure to nail the pronunciation. New York, it was clear, did not suffer fools gladly, be they bus drivers who fail to yield the right-of-way, or interlopers from the South with a lame French accent.

The next day we set out for the Fair itself. The highlight that I remember best was Michelangelo's Pieta, the statue of Mary holding the body of her crucified Son, a feature of the pavilion from the Vatican. The line to see it snaked around the building, but we persisted there for over an hour, though our view of the sculpture lasted just a few seconds. All of us onlookers were on a moving floor, like a conveyor belt, that made sure no gawkers dallied.

We also got a glimpse, even shorter than the one of the renowned work of art, of probably the most famous New Yorker of that time: Johnny Carson. Surrounded by a phalanx of courtiers, the late-night talk show host, known for his dislike of public appearances, was grinning broadly when we saw him, perhaps happy that he seemed to be exiting the scene. Mike and I saw one other thing at the Fair that was another kind of celebrity: a Belgian waffle.

Neither of us had heard of such a viand prior to going to New York, but it was the talk heard in the crowd virtually wherever we went: "Have you seen (eaten, bought) a Belgian waffle?" Twice or thrice the thickness of the conventional breakfast treat, the Belgian version was topped with a pile of whipped cream and strawberries. We came, we saw, but we didn't buy.

Either that day or the next, my pal and roomie (both at the sem and the G.W.) bailed me out of a fix while we were at the Fair. I was wearing Bermuda shorts, apparently either too old or too small. Whichever was the case, some unremembered movement caused them to rip right down the seam on my backside. The sound and then the ventilation let me know immediately that I was going to be the laughingstock of the 1964 World's Fair. There was no way I could continue walking about and make a spectacle of myself. I told Mike that I was sorry, but we'd just have to leave. I wasn't about to expose my backside to tens of thousands of people. That's when his stroke of genius came from his lips like a thunderclap: "Just pull out your shirt. That will cover it up." That we enjoyed the rest of our day at the Fair we owe to his...what's that they call it? Oh, yes, common sense.

Scholarly fellows that we were, on the next day Mike and I visited the New York Public Library, just for the fun that libraries yield to those who know where to find it. You may recall that libraries once had what were called "card catalogues," skinny, deep drawers that housed, on index cards, information about titles, authors, and where books could be found. I had heard that this library had an enormous collection of books by and about William Shakespeare, and I was just about to count how many drawers were devoted to the Bard when around the corner came Joe Flahaven, the only person Mike and I knew who lived in New York.

Joe had come, during the school year just completed, to St. John's by way of Brooklyn, and we knew him slightly, but not well enough to alert him to our travel plans or to make an attempt to rendezvous with him on our arrival. It surprised us both when Joe, without consulting his parents (no cell phone) invited us to complete our New York stay at their apartment. We declined, of course, but he was insistent, and we finally were persuaded to accept.

We returned to the George Washington, packed our suitcases, and went to the desk to check out. I asked for a refund for the two days that we wouldn't be staying because of our early departure. The desk clerk refused. It was from my father, I'm sure, that a certain stubbornness of nature came to exist in me. So I didn't take the clerk's "no" for an answer. He was resistant to my pleas, arguments, and finally I resorted to a threat: "I'm going to report you to the Better Business Bureau." He didn't seem to care. I thrust a dollar at him for change to make a phone call from a booth directly across the lobby from the clerk's desk. He provided me with change.

Finding the Bureau's number in the directory within the booth, which was cut off from the lobby by its closed door, I dialed and spoke to the representative of the B.B.B. He told me I was out of luck. I pleaded with him to see the injustice of the situation. No soap. I hung up and went to the desk. "What did they say?" inquired the clerk.

"He told me to call him back, and it would all be settled," I prevaricated. I don't know why that worked, but the clerk was quickly refunding $40, the fee for two nights. When he got to thirty-five dollars, he asked, "Will you take thirty-five?" I demanded and got it all, filling Mike in on my imaginary conversation with the Better Business guy as we left the hotel. We were off to Brooklyn.

Joe's mother and father acted as if taking in two Arkies without being consulted by their son was the most natural thing in the world, and they were generous hosts for two nights, on one of which we went to Fort Hamilton, an army base (Joe's dad was retired from the military) located in Brooklyn, where we enjoyed the bounty of a Sunday-night officers' dinner. The offerings ranged from roast beef to multiple kinds of fish, and neither Mike nor I had ever seen caviar at a buffet, much less multiple kinds and colors of it.

Our trip back to Little Rock was complicated before it even got underway because I couldn't find my bus ticket. I had stored it in my suitcase, and it just wasn't there. I suspected theft (NOT by the Flahavens!), but suspicion was all I had. So Mike and I joined forces to purchase a one-way ticket to the capital of Arkansas, and we made it back within a day's time.

You probably remember my mention of my father's "bull-headedness," as he called it. He spent more than a year badgering Greyhound to refund my money for the return trip when it was clear that my ticket—the number of which was determined from Mike's ticket, which he had purchased just after I had gotten mine—had never been used or cashed in. Sending certified letters to the president of the bus line, Dad finally wore Greyhound down, and I was the surprised recipient of a check from the company.

The journey had multiple small highlights, including meeting the same homeless guy on two different nights in two different parts of town, once requesting money so he could "buy gasoline to burn that building down." We didn't contribute. I took a picture of Mike while we were waiting for a subway, getting him to move just in front of the sign indicating Broad Street. When I had it developed, and he saw the sign in the background, I told him, "That's as close to one (a *broad*) that you got the entire trip." A first for both of us was seeing a homosexual couple holding hands and kissing, and along with that, noticing a man in a bar shaking his head at us, saying, "Don't do it to each other," thinking we were gay. Well, the trip made us happy but not gay.

*

Later that summer, Mike and Al and I were working in the seminary library with Father Benz as our boss. We spent most of the time in a room where books were labeled on their spines with their Library of Congress number. The work was indoors, in air-conditioned protection from the Arkansas heat and humidity—so it was a good job. Adding to the air-cooled comfort was a radio tuned to a local FM station. "Easy listening" were the by-words in those days for virtually anything that wasn't Rock and Roll, and it was the station that Father Benz had picked to hear. His library, his radio, his station.

FM ("frequency modulation," whatever that means) stations, at least in those days, were known for two things: better sound than AM stations (to provide equal time, I looked it up: "amplitude modulation") but for much shorter range of its signal. People sometimes complained that even local FM stations sometimes sent out weak signals.

All that technical data having been given, I finally get to the point. As the three of us worked and Perry Como (ask your grandmother) sang, we heard a kind of hiccup and then the music resumed, but Perry, who hadn't finished "Catch a Falling Star," had been replaced by some other artist. It was odd. The music that continued was of the same ilk, and we thought no more about it until the announcer, who also had replaced the one we had been listening to, told us that it was 11:15, an hour later than our watches showed, then added station call letters different from our Little Rock station, and finally noted his location, a town somewhere in New Jersey. We Little Rock listeners then "looked at each other with a wild surmise," as Mr. Keats once wrote of some other guys who were left guessing.

*

Later that summer Al and I were, for reasons now not exactly clear to me, sitting in the prep side residence of one of the two priests who lived in that building. Why we were there isn't the point of the story, so I'll get on with the narrative to say that we heard a noise coming from the next room, which was the priest's bedroom. The priest was gone, so it was up to us to investigate.

We entered, deliberately (fearfully?) and listened for the sound. We heard it again. Perhaps it was coming from the clothes closet. Nothing there. Then we heard it again—at or below our knees. In an empty, metal wastebasket was a mouse. The wastebasket was close to nothing that would explain how the mouse got within. A dresser was probably at least a yard away. Surely a mouse couldn't swan dive that far! And the sides of the wastebasket were slick; how could it have climbed up that metallic wall?

We had no explanation for any of it. I asked Al what he thought we should do with the critter. Remember, Al was the guy who built and set the trap that snared the rat. He picked up the wastebasket decisively. I followed him out of the priest's room. Where was he going?

When he got to the "jakes," he took a sharp turn into them. Is he going to flush the little fellow down the toilet? That struck me as a pretty ugly way to go. Though it was absolutely a close relative of that thieving, unattractive rat, he was so much smaller and, dare I say it, cuter, that I was hoping that Al didn't have a successful rodent drowning in mind. He didn't.

He strode to the window, the fourth floor window, I should add, and before I could say, "Don't!" he gave the basket a shake as his arm extended out the window. We leaned out the window to see the furry little ball descending, at thirty-two feet per second, per second, and it quickly made contact with the sidewalk below. It took less than a half-second for it to get into high gear, scampering for the woods, not slowed in the slightest by its crash landing. Al just grinned as we drew out heads back into the room. The boy knew more about rats and mice than anybody else I had ever known.

Years later, when teaching boys at Catholic High School a poem by Walt Whitman that featured the line, "a mouse is miracle enough to stagger sextillions of infidels," I would, to validate Walt's point, always tell my miracle mouse tale.

*

Tom Krone, a younger-than-I seminarian from Fort Smith, and I were assigned to assist a priest who was conducting a summer retreat for women. We carried suitcases from the retreatants' cars to their rooms on Friday night and carried out other tasks over the weekend until the retreat ended on Sunday morning after Mass. The retreat master was a veteran local priest, an amiable man who was that evening going to give the first of several talks and then conduct Benediction of the Blessed Sacrament, a service whereby a consecrated host in a container called a monstrance is put on display. The monstrance is a vessel on a stand perhaps two feet tall with a starburst shape at the top into which the host is placed behind a glass cover.

Before the Benediction service, which was to be held about 9:00 p.m., after his talk in the seminary main chapel, the priest asked Tom and me about the altar lighting and if we could, at the end of the Benediction, turn off certain lights in the chapel. We said we could.

When Benediction was concluded, but with the women still present in the chapel and the monstrance remaining on the altar, Tom and I, who had been assisting at the service, exited the altar area to go behind it, and we began to turn off the lights that the priest had identified. We returned to the altar and found that our efforts had left the seating area of the chapel in complete darkness, the twenty or so women invisible from the altar. The lone light in the cavernous room was directly above the monstrance. Tom and I took our places next to the priest, who was kneeling facing the monstrance. He knelt in silence for what I thought was an uncomfortably long time. What was going on? Finally, he said in a strong and seemingly heartfelt voice, "Good night, sweet Jesus!"

We left the altar. The women could be heard bumping into their pews as they departed. Tom's later description of it all was both succinct and apt: "Spooky."

*

The young priests at St. John's inspired many of us to view the church's role in promoting civil rights as an important one. When some of my St. John's fellows told me they were heading to Mississippi to become part of a march to protest the shooting of a black civil rights activist, I signed on. James Meredith had been shot while attempting to carry out his "March Against Fear," a trek from Memphis to Jackson, Mississippi.

We were Johnnies-Come-Lately to the march, as we couldn't get to it until the night before it ended. The 220 miles between Memphis and Jackson had been traversed by thousands who took Meredith's place. When we joined up on Saturday night, at Tougaloo College, just a few miles from the state capitol which was the intended destination, we met people who had been on the march for more than one hundred miles. I met a young man, in his late teens or early twenties, the side of whose face looked like it had been gouged with a cheese grater. Actually, it was worse than that. In a town called Canton, Mississippi, state police attacked and tear-gassed the marchers, and he had been dragged across a parking lot, with his face being the primary contact between him and the concrete. Bad as he looked, he was almost feisty in his assertion that the non-violence to which the marchers had pledged themselves was an effective weapon. "We're kicking their asses," he figuratively proclaimed, which was his view of the effect that the march was having on the sentiments of Americans as a whole versus those who were handing out physical punishment. He looked more like the "kickee" than the "kicker," but I understood what he meant.

That Saturday night a final pep rally of sorts was held, with speeches and music to fire up the marchers for the last push into Jackson. The actor Paul Newman spoke, telling the marchers that people all across the country, seeing on TV the violence that had been employed, first against James Meredith, and then against them, had decided that those protecting the racist agenda were on the wrong side of history. James Brown, "the hardest working man in show business," sang long and loud, and the crowd was primed for the remaining miles to come.

I remember that on the walk to Jackson a rumor went up and down the line: "The Klan is in the woods with rifles." Off to our left was, indeed, a dense forest, but happily no gunfire erupted on the way. Even though it was the March Against Fear, the thought that someone had me in his rifle sights was scary.

We passed through a neighborhood in Jackson that was virtually all-black, and even though residents waved to us from their front porches, they were too afraid to join the march as they were being urged to do. They had to live there; we would be returning home.

I saw Dr. Martin Luther King leading a group of ministers and priests, and when we got to the state capitol in Jackson, it was surrounded by state policemen and forest rangers and others in uniform, all bearing rifles and shotguns. No protester was going to set foot on the grounds of the state capitol of Mississippi! So we surrounded the building and sang "We Shall Overcome" to all those armed men, and somebody gave a short speech through a bullhorn, and the March Against Fear was over.

FIDEM SCIT

V • VALEDICTORY

I hope you can tell that I have great affection for my St. John's experience and for the boys and men I met and came to know there. The four years I spent there have positively affected me, and I'm grateful for them. If the events and people I have depicted don't fit with anyone's image of what seminarians are or should have been, I can only say that I found them to be admirable people who in some cases made excellent priests and in others excellent laymen.

When my son, John, was about ten, approximately fifteen years after I had been a student there, and a dozen years after the seminary had closed, I took him on a Sunday afternoon to St. John's, about which I had told him a few stories. We saw no one else that day. Not surprising to me, we found several doors open. We walked in to Fletcher Hall, the newest of the residence halls, and toured the ground floor, which included a chapel. I took John to the sacristy, where a priest would put on his vestments before

Mass. I opened a cabinet where once upon a time chalices would have been kept. Again, I wasn't too shocked to see several of the gold-lined and quite valuable chalices on the shelf. St. John's, in my mind, was always a bit of a loose ship.

Next we entered Morris Hall, the main building. We went down a level to the library and found it open, though the books had long before been sold. At the rear of the library, where Mike and Al and I had heard New Jersey on the radio, was a stairwell that led up to the chapel above. It turned out that the door at the top of the stairs was locked and we couldn't get entry to the chapel. But before we got to the top, I saw lying on a stair a folded sheet of paper, clean, unwrinkled, looking as if just dropped there. Opening it, I recognized a Work Day Duty sheet, a weekly publication in my day and in years before and after, identifying what job each seminarian was expected to perform on Work Day. I looked at the list. Typed alongside the assignment to "rake leaves" was my name.

I think Tom Krone's description applies: *spooky*.

THE END

Made in the USA
San Bernardino, CA
25 June 2017